LUSITANIA

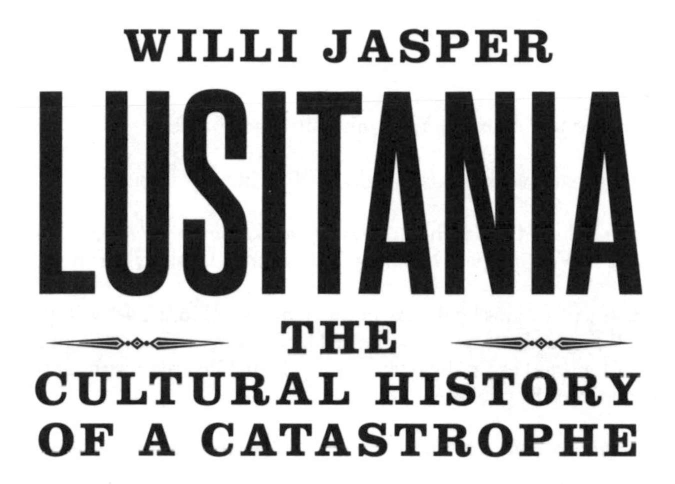

Translated by Stewart Spencer

YALE UNIVERSITY PRESS
NEW HAVEN AND LONDON

First published in English by Yale University Press in 2016

For information about this and other Yale University Press publications, please contact:

U.S. Office: sales.press@yale.edu yalebooks.com
Europe Office: sales@yaleup.co.uk yalebooks.co.uk

Typeset in Adobe Caslon Pro by IDSUK (DataConnection) Ltd
Printed in Great Britain by Gomer Press, Llandysul, Ceredigion, Wales

Library of Congress Cataloging-in-Publication Data

Names: Jasper, Willi, author. | Spencer, Stewart, translator.
Title: Lusitania : the cultural history of a catastrophe / Willi Jasper ; translated by Stewart Spencer.
Other titles: Lusitania. English
Description: New Haven : Yale University Press, [2016] | Originally published: Jasper, Willi. Lusitania : Kulturgeschichte einer Katastrophe. Berlin : be.bra verlag GmbH, 2015. | Includes bibliographical references and index.
Identifiers: LCCN 2016010335 | ISBN 9780300221381 (alk. paper)
Subjects: LCSH: Lusitania (Steamship) | World War, 1914–1918—Naval operations—Submarine. | World War, 1914–1918--Moral and ethical aspects.
Classification: LCC D592.L8 J37 2016 | DDC 940.4/514—dc23
LC record available at http://lccn.loc.gov/2016010335

A catalogue record for this book is available from the British Library.

10 9 8 7 6 5 4 3 2 1

Contents

Introduction

The Old Head of Kinsale is an outcrop of hard sandstone rock projecting into the Atlantic on Ireland's south-west coast and presents a fascinating spectacle. With its ruined buildings and a lighthouse visible for miles around, its archaic landscape is a potent reminder of Celtic history and its maritime myths. The pounding waves and the gusting winds, which recall nothing so much as the harmony of the spheres, seem to the listener to be the songs of primeval spirits. Even the worldly American golf club that has had an eighteen-hole course here since 1997 has been unable to destroy this mysterious atmosphere. For over two thousand years the Old Head of Kinsale has been first and foremost a viewing platform for coastguards and a landmark for passing seafarers. A beacon is believed to have been located on the headland even in pre-Christian times. By the seventeenth century its duties had been taken over by a simple cottage with an open coal fire in a brazier on its roof, and by 1853 this building had been replaced in turn by a lighthouse whose fixed white light – a multi-concentric wick oil lamp – was positioned at a height of 236 feet (72 metres) above high water. And yet this romantic spot has not always been so peaceful and idyllic, for it also recalls a whole host of appalling maritime disasters.

In September 1588, for example, thousands of soldiers from the Spanish Armada were shipwrecked both here and along the Scottish coast, losing almost half of their ships. Sailors and soldiers drowned below deck or capsized in their landing craft. Others leapt overboard and disappeared without trace. In the raging sea, desperate mariners clung to barrels and beams. Whipped up by the wind and the waves, flotsam and jetsam smashed into their bodies, while the weight of the gold chains and gold purses worn by captains, officers and Catholic dignitaries proved to be their undoing. It was not so much the English cannon as the powerful storm with its towering waves that sank the ponderous Spanish galleons and scattered wreckage and bodies along the Irish coastline from Bantry Bay to the Old Head of Kinsale. Along the shoreline locals gathered with soldiers loyal to the English queen, who also reigned over Ireland at this date in the country's history. A number of them danced for joy at the defeat of the Spaniards, while others cursed the Protestants' naval might.

But it is above all the modern tragedies of the two British ocean-going liners, the *Titanic* and the *Lusitania*, that are rooted in the memories of the inhabitants of this coastal region. For both vessels the lighthouse on the Old Head of Kinsale was to prove a deceptive beacon, initially signalling not only the hopes bound up with the vessels' departure for the New World but also the joy of arriving back in Europe. Not only cemeteries, museums and monuments serve as a constant reminder of these legendary liners, so too do tourist shops, pubs, hotels and restaurants. The centre of this cult of memory is the harbour town of Cobh, formerly known as Queenstown, with its museum dedicated to the history of the Irish diaspora, the Cobh Heritage Centre, as well as an organized 'Titanic Trail', a monumental memorial to the victims of the *Lusitania* disaster and the marked graves that lie in the Clonmel Cemetery.

Cobh was the last port of call of the *Titanic* on her ill-fated voyage across the Atlantic and was also the town where most of the victims of the *Lusitania* disaster were buried. It was here, too, that almost half of the six million Irish men, women and children who emigrated during the last two centuries boarded vessels taking them away from the country of their birth. The *Titanic* also included a sizeable group of émigrés among her third-class passengers. When the vessel passed the Old Head lighthouse on 11 April 1912, her passengers waved to the shore, little suspecting that they would never see land again: declared unsinkable, the *Titanic* never reached her destination in New York but sank after striking an iceberg during the night of 14–15 April, disappearing into almost 12,000 feet of icy water off the coast of Newfoundland and remaining indelibly etched on the collective subconscious of contemporaries and later generations alike. Of the 2,207 passengers and crew who had been on board at the time of the accident, only 712 survived.

Whereas earlier maritime disasters had failed to provide the stuff of legend, the tragedy associated with the sinking of the *Titanic* became a tale about modern man. Even

Germany – Britain's principal competitor on the transatlantic route – was touched by the disaster. 'The worst maritime accident in the whole of human history is one that affects the whole of humankind,' wrote the *Hamburger Fremdenblatt*, while also expressing the hope that our 'Promethean aspirations' would not be discouraged and that no 'blows of fate' would deter us from 'believing in progress' and 'defeating the forces of nature'.[1]

Three years later an equally tragic event unfolded only 11 nautical miles off the Old Head of Kinsale, when the *Lusitania* was on her way from New York to Liverpool. She, too, was flying the Union Jack and in terms of her size, technology and fittings was entirely comparable to the *Titanic*. But the events leading up to her loss and the circumstances surrounding it were different, its consequences even more catastrophic. By 1915 the world had been at war for several months and more was at stake than merely the peacetime technological rivalry between nations attempting to 'defeat the forces of nature'. The peoples of Europe were engaged in a murderous rivalry fuelling weapons production and aimed at greater efficiency in the mass destruction of their fellow human beings. German submarines were now the most important and sinister weapon in the armoury of the head of the German Navy, Alfred von Tirpitz, their particular goal being to break through the British naval blockade. Civilian vessels, too, were at risk from the Germans' unrestricted U-boat war.

The fatal encounter between the *U-20* and the *Lusitania* took place off the Irish coast at around 2.10 pm on 7 May

1915, when the captain of the German submarine gave the order to fire without any preliminary warning. The torpedo struck the liner on her starboard side, just behind her bridge and between her first and second smokestacks. Shortly afterwards there was a second explosion deep inside the ship, which immediately began to list. Within eighteen minutes she had sunk. The *Titanic*, by contrast, needed almost three hours to capsize. On the doomed *Lusitania* there was scarcely time to launch the lifeboats. Instead there was an unimaginable state of panic, during which a number of lifeboats overturned, burying their occupants beneath them, while other passengers leapt into the cold water without lifejackets. One first-class passenger, Michael G. Byrne, who was a native of County Kilkenny but who in 1915 was working as a special deputy sheriff in New York, told a reporter that

> When I saw no chance of a lifeboat [. . .], I then jumped into the sea as the ship was just going down. I swam about for two hours among dead and live bodies and floating wreckage. [. . .] I still think I see the struggling of the poor passengers in the water. Poor little children in the arms of their mothers tightly grasped in death floating on the surface of the sea. The dying cries are still in my ears and the sight of the struggle for life through the deep sea will remain forever in my memory. The hideous howl of the *Lusitania* as she was swallowed in the waves brings a dismal thrill all over me.[2]

Some 1,197 passengers and crew lost their lives, among them were 270 women and infants. Of the total dead, 128 were American citizens.

While the passengers jumped to their deaths and the sea slowly filled with bodies and body parts, the German U-boat captain observed the scene through his periscope. When he had seen all that he needed to see, he gave orders for his vessel to dive. The cold-blooded torpedoing of a huge passenger liner without any advance warning was unprecedented. The fact that the *Lusitania* was named after an ancient Spanish province and recalled the naval battle of 1588 was not without a certain macabre historical symbolism.

In Germany, the sinking of the *Titanic* had provoked feelings of shock and dismay, whereas the response to the loss of the *Lusitania* was for the most part jubilation. From his military headquarters at Stenay in north-west France Crown Prince Wilhelm cabled to his father, Kaiser Wilhelm: 'Tremendous delight here at the torpedoing of the *Lusitania*. [. . .] The more ruthlessly the U-boat war is waged, the quicker the war will end.'[3] Many German newspapers struck a similarly triumphalist note. Take the *Westfälische Tageszeitung*: 'Our U-boats have finally made a significant catch. [. . .] We Germans are heartily pleased at this successful blow and regard with a wry smile the general howls of anger and screams of indignation. [. . .] No sentimentality: just a fight to the finish with this nation of vulgar shopkeepers.'[4] Even Thomas Mann joined in the bloodcurdling chorus of jubilation triggered by the sinking of the *Lusitania*.

Conversely, news of the disaster was greeted with disbelief in Great Britain, the United States and other members of the Entente and even in neutral nations. There was boundless indignation at the appalling human scale of the disaster, a sense of outrage felt in the most disparate political camps and surpassed only by the feeling of horror that there was no longer any distinction between combatants and civilians. The president of the University of Virginia, Edwin Alderman, summed up American reactions when he spoke of the numb astonishment at the realization that the actions of a great nation could be marked by such brutality and cruelty.[5] Magazines published front-page cartoons showing drowned children as ghosts chastising the German Kaiser, and pent-up emotions found expression throughout the English-speaking world in anti-German riots.

Prior to the sinking of the *Lusitania* there are been no organized political force in the United States that advocated the country's involvement in the war, but the deaths of 128 Americans changed the political climate in a starkly dramatic way. Countless Americans joined the ranks of the militants overnight: in their eyes conflict between American democracy and German autocracy had now become inevitable.

The sinking of the *Lusitania* has exercised the minds of scholars and of the general public for a century, and yet there are still a number of important questions that remain unanswered. Significantly, until now it is only Anglo-Saxon writers who have dealt with the subject. And in almost every case they have been concerned to prove or disprove conspiracy theories, notably the role of Winston Churchill, who was First Lord of the Admiralty in 1915 and who has been accused of deliberately staging the tragedy in order to incite the Americans against Germany. Divers have explored the wreck of the *Lusitania* at great expense – and in the glare of widespread publicity – in the hope of discovering incriminating munitions chests or other evidence of violations of the rules of war. But the debate continues to go round in circles. There is still the need for a comprehensive assessment of the cultural history of the disaster – especially from a German perspective – even though the sinking of the *Lusitania* was of greater symbolic and concrete significance for the shift in the dynamics of the war than any other event. What was involved here was more than merely the increase in the number of combatants and areas of conflict, but, above all, a new ideological, moral and religious dimension to the battle between 'German culture' and 'western civilization'. The fatal belief that the Germans had a cultural mission in life grew increasingly radicalized, as did the religious convictions of educated Germans. If we share the view of the American diplomat and historian George F. Kennan that the First World War was the 'seminal catastrophe' of the twentieth century,[6] we may well conclude that the sinking of the *Lusitania* was the 'seminal catastrophe' of both world wars, marking, as it did, the beginning of a process whereby totalitarian violence lost all of its inhibitions and raged completely out of control.

CHAPTER 1

Report to Noah

Ship Owners and Admirals

Even the planning and building of the *Lusitania* were a reflection of the militant rivalry between the major powers. By the beginning of the twentieth century, Britain, which had been the leading maritime nation since the end of the seventeenth century, was beginning to see its international hegemony challenged by self-aggrandizing states such as the German Reich and the United States of America. Among its rivals were not only the Hamburg-Amerika-Line (HAPAG) and the Norddeutscher Lloyd but, more especially, the imperialist aspirations of the American banker John Pierpont Morgan, who was keen to contest the British monopoly in international shipping. A major step in this direction was his acquisition of the White Star Line in 1902. It was the Cunard Line that felt most threatened by Morgan's monopolistic ambitions. The Cunard Line had been founded in 1840 by the Canadian businessman Samuel Cunard and by a number of wealthy backers. Based in Southampton, it was initially known as the British and North American Royal Mail Steam-Packet Company and commanded a fleet of four paddle-steamers – the *Britannia*, *Acadia*, *Caledonia* and *Columbia* – that not only ferried post between Great Britain and America but soon developed into an international company dealing in passenger and freight transport, becoming a limited liability company in 1877, when it took the name of the Cunard Steamship Company Ltd. It enjoyed a solid reputation in émigré circles not least as a result of developments in steamship technology that played a significant role in improving the lot of emigrants.

The Irish potato famine of the 1840s that was caused by the mismanagement and capriciousness of the country's major landowners had led hundreds of thousands of Irish men and women to leave their native land, many of them sailing to the United States in conditions that can only be described as appalling: not infrequently they were forced to entrust themselves to what became known as 'floating coffins' – there were enough unscrupulous shipowners keen to exploit the plight of impoverished Irishmen and women by using wooden and barely seaworthy windjammers to transport their passengers to a new life overseas. Travellers were packed like cattle in the narrow space between decks and forced to endure a perilous and unpleasant journey which, depending on the weather, could last between forty and eighty days. Between 1847 and 1853 no fewer than sixty emigrant vessels sank on their way from England or Ireland to America. And even if these rotting hulks reached their destination, their passengers still ran the risk of succumbing to typhus, cholera and dysentery as a result of the inadequate hygiene and poor food on board.

The technological progress represented by ironclad steamers made a not inconsiderable difference to anyone wanting to emigrate. Travellers were no longer at the mercy of the wind and weather, while the conditions on board were now much more humane. Cunard's first paddle-steamer to be built from iron was the *Persia*. Launched in 1855, she had already won the Blue Riband for the fastest Atlantic crossing by April 1856, achieving an average speed of 13.46 knots. According to an enthusiastic report in the German-language *Polytechnisches Journal*, she had 'a tonnage of 3,600 grt' and provided 'comfortable accommodation for 260 saloon-class passengers'. The writer was particularly impressed by the reliability of the vessel with its enormous paddle-wheels, a vessel well calculated to confirm the reputation of the Cunard Line,

> whose ships can complete the crossing between Liverpool and New York in approximately ten days and do so, moreover, with such punctuality that if one of these vessels misses its appointed time of arrival by even so much as an hour, there is an immediate sense of disquiet in the business world in London, Liverpool, Manchester and elsewhere. It is the largest steamship afloat in the world and among the company's fleet the first to be constructed from iron – out of consideration for the fact that these ships might one day be used for the purposes of war, the British government previously refused to allow such ships to be made from iron, a view that has now only gradually been abandoned.[1]

By the end of the nineteenth century, the time taken to cross the Atlantic had been further reduced to between six and seven days, and it was Cunard vessels that played a significant role in capturing these records: in 1894, for example, it was the *Lucania* that received the Blue Riband. British pride was badly dented when in 1897 – the year of Queen Victoria's diamond jubilee – this coveted trophy passed to a German liner, the *Kaiser Wilhelm der Große*. (Three years later the Blue Riband was awarded to another German liner, HAPAG's *Deutschland*.) The Cunard chairman, Lord Inverclyde, reacted to this perceived humiliation by asking the British government for more effective financial support. The Admiralty also supported the request, since it hoped that a fleet of new and faster ships would prove useful. On 13 August 1903 the Lower House of Parliament agreed to provide a loan of £2.6m to build two modern ships. The loan was offered at a low interest rate and did not need to be repaid for twenty years. At the same time the Admiralty signed a secret accord with Cunard, thereby securing its own military interests. The main terms of this secret agreement concerned metal plating to protect the engines and the company's willingness to make the ships available in the event of war. In order to protect the vessels from enemy shells, all the important technical installations were to be below the waterline and additionally shielded by coal bunkers positioned in front of them.

The naval architect Leonard Peskett was entrusted with the task of designing the two new vessels, of which the *Lusitania* was built by John Brown & Company on the

Clyde, while her sister ship, the *Mauretania*, was built by Swan Hunter at Newcastle upon Tyne. It went without saying that the two liners were intended to be the largest, fastest and most luxurious in the world. This was also the first time that the new steam-turbine technology had been used in ships of this size, while the four triple-bladed propellers also marked a departure from the traditional design. The technical specifications and the dimensions of both ships were almost identical.

The *Lusitania* was launched on 7 June 1906, five months before her sister ship. She could accommodate 2,000 passengers and a crew of 850 and was at this date the world's biggest passenger liner, 787 feet (239.9 metres) in length, with a beam of 87 feet (26.5 metres), a displacement of 44,767 tons and four direct-acting steam turbines producing 76,000 hp. The turbines were driven by a total of twenty-five boilers, which consumed some 1,000 tons of coal a day, which in turn meant that they had to be cooled with 250,000 litres of water a minute. Speed being of the essence, Cunard demanded a top speed of 24.5 knots. For every tenth of a knot that the ship fell short of this target, the shipbuilders would incur a fine of £10,000. But even on the vessel's first sea trial in the Irish Sea, she reached a speed of 26.4 knots, albeit with an unacceptable side-effect due to a defect in the ship's construction: at this speed, the stern began to vibrate violently and steel plates and supports were so badly shaken as to render the second-class accommodation uninhabitable.

Within a month the engineers had added internal stiffening to the stern of the ship. In the end a total of four million rivets held the liner together and reduced the level of vibration – the *Titanic* required only three million rivets when she was built a few years later.

In terms of speed and manoeuvrability the *Lusitania* was in a class of her own. Her turning circle was only 2,850 feet (870 metres), compared with the *Titanic*'s 3,855 feet (1,175 metres). Experts were particularly impressed by the fact that bulkheads could seal off the lower part of the ship and make her watertight at the press of an electric button. As a result, the *Lusitania* was 'as unsinkable as a ship can be', to quote the *New York Times*.[2] Similar claims had been made for the *Titanic*, but Robert D. Ballard, who discovered the wreck of the *Titanic*, believes that the *Lusitania* was in fact the more stable of the two vessels and that she would have survived a comparable collision with an iceberg.[3]

Two different designers were responsible for the interiors of both vessels: the Scotsman James Miller was commissioned to design the interior of the *Lusitania*, Harold A. Peto, who was in fact better known as a land-scape gardener, that of the *Mauretania*. Both men were at pains to provide the best possible materials, designs and craftsmanship. African mahogany, French walnut, Austrian oak and Spanish plane were used for the first- and second-class staterooms.

With his dark wood panelling for the *Mauretania*, Peto stressed the conservative British tradition, whereas Miller took his cue from Italian and French models, preferring to use white, notably in the first-class dining saloon, whose white and gold decor and stucco dome clearly recall Louis

XIV's Petit Trianon at Versailles. The other staterooms on the first-class deck had huge barrel-vaulted skylights with stained glass windows that allowed strangely coloured light to enter. The Veranda Café with its plants and potted palms resembled nothing so much as an elegant Mediterranean street café, while the foyer, smoking room, lounge (complete with Palm Court Orchestra) and, above all, the two Royal Suites that featured two bedrooms, en suite bathroom, separate water closet and even a private dining room and private saloon, could stand comparison with any luxury hotel. This inevitably came at a price: for a one-way ticket in the Royal Suite Cunard charged $4,000, more than one hundred times the average wage at this period.

Even the second-class accommodation in the rear of the vessel created a dazzling impression with its vaulted dining saloon, smoking room and a reading room 'for ladies', while the third-class accommodation at the front of the ship had separate public areas, although here the cabins, each with between four and six beds, may have seemed relatively spartan when compared to the luxury of their first-class equivalents. Yet in comparison to the unhygienic mass accommodation between decks in the older ships, these new arrangements undoubtedly represented a significant improvement in terms of passenger comfort. In the liner's vast galleys, with their additional kitchenettes, bakeries, pantries and larders, as many as 10,000 meals were prepared every day. The food for the first- and second-class passengers may have differed from that of the third class in respect of the care that went into its presentation, but its quality was in no way superior, for even in third class nutritious food was guaranteed. Free medical care was available to all passengers. There was a ship's hospital with four wards and even an isolation unit for infectious diseases. Pregnant emigrants often planned their transatlantic crossing to coincide with the birth of their child, allowing them to take advantage of the *Lusitania*'s obstetric facilities. On the occasion of the liner's maiden voyage in 1907, this unusual combination of luxury and mutual support prompted the United States senator George Sutherland to describe the *Lusitania* as 'more beautiful than Solomon's Temple and large enough to hold all his wives and mothers-in-law'.[4]

When the much-admired liner left Liverpool on her first major voyage on the evening of 7 September 1907, thousands of cheering men and women had gathered on the quayside with a large number of journalists, all of them hoping that the *Lusitania* would recapture the Blue Riband on her maiden voyage, but unexpectedly bad weather prevented her from wresting back the trophy from the *Deutschland*. But by the time the *Lusitania* docked in New York on 13 September, she had missed the record by only thirty minutes. In New York, too, there were scenes of jubilation, and when the general public was allowed to tour the vessel prior to her return to Europe, the crowds were almost uncontrollable.

Among those who came to admire the *Lusitania* was Mark Twain, whose enthusiasm for the vessel's safety standards had a positively mythic ring: 'I guess I'll have to tell Noah about it when I see him.'[5] The world-famous writer could draw on his own experiences as a river-boat pilot on a Mississippi steamship and had even created a pen-name for himself as a conscious borrowing from shipboard slang – 'Mark Twain' was a signal meaning 'by the mark two fathoms'. His reference to Noah's Ark was not just intended as praise of modern technology and of the multicultural milieu on board the *Lusitania* but was also deliberately designed to recall the ambiguity of the biblical word 'ark', meaning both 'palace' and 'coffin'.

The *Lusitania* captured the Blue Riband on her second transatlantic crossing, in October 1907, achieving an average speed of over twenty-four knots and requiring under five days to complete the journey. Four weeks later the press reported on a second record that the liner had broken, this one concerning the value of her cargo, for in November 1907 the ship transported twenty tons of gold worth £2.5m (around €650m at today's prices) across the ocean. In February 1909 the *Lusitania* had an opportunity to prove that she was a safe 'ark' in the first sense intended by Mark Twain, when she arrived in New York two days later than planned after encountering 75-feet waves in mid-ocean. Although the starboard anchor was lost and the command bridge and parts of the superstructure and radio antenna were damaged, the crew and passengers suffered only shock. The liner's reputation as 'unsinkable' was now fully established. Her only rival was her sister ship, the *Mauretania*, which captured the Blue Riband in September 1909, a family rivalry that in no way harmed the company's business interests. For Cunard, the situation changed only in 1910–11, when the White Star Line built the *Olympic* and the *Titanic*, two liners whose size and interiors set new standards, even if their deployment was to prove ill-fated from the outset.

During her sea trials, the *Olympic* rammed the harbour wall at Liverpool – her captain on that occasion was Edward John Smith, who was to assume command of the *Titanic* on her fateful maiden voyage in 1912. And in September 1911 the *Olympic* collided with a battleship, the HMS *Hawke*, off the Isle of Wight, requiring several months of repair work and delaying the completion of the *Titanic*, whose maiden voyage began on 10 April 1912, famously ending four days later, when she collided with an iceberg.

The Myth of the *Titanic*

Why did Germany lament the loss of the *Titanic* but celebrate the sinking of the *Lusitania*? The *Titanic* was not unique but became so only as a result of the myths that attached themselves to the ship like barnacles. But how did these myths originate? What was so 'mythical' about the sinking of the *Titanic*? Accidents suffered by passenger liners on the North Atlantic route and even collisions with icebergs were by no means exceptional at this period. In 1903 alone, twenty relatively large vessels collided with icebergs, and twelve of them sank. In 1907 the German liner *Kronprinz Wilhelm* found herself unexpectedly in an ice field but managed to extricate herself with only a few scratches and bumps. And we have almost completely forgotten the fate of the *Empress of Ireland*, which collided with the Norwegian freighter *Storstad* in the St Lawrence River on 29 May 1914 and sank with the loss of 1,012 lives. In spite of the magnitude of this last-named tragedy, it was not a disaster that shook the world and as such was unsuited to forming the basis of a legend. Rather, it was the outbreak of the First World War only four weeks later that became the focus of interest of newspapers and telegraph offices throughout the entire world.

The tragedy of the *Titanic*, conversely, unfolded at a time that was better suited to catching the spirit of the age, the drama of its loss coming to be regarded as an exemplary illustration of the ancient myth of man's futile struggle with the forces of nature. The White Star Line had declared the *Titanic* to be the unsinkable flagship of progress, and yet she, too, was subject to the immutable historical law that ship and shipwreck form a symbolic entity.

The ship is one of humankind's most significant inventions. Nevertheless, the story of seafaring is not only one of successful conquest and trade but also a tale of tragedy and failure in the form of shipwrecks. The kinship between success and failure was clear from an early date: in the winter of 1492, for example, Christopher Columbus cursed his flagship *Santa Maria* for her vulnerability during his first voyage of discovery – he was lucky to be able to return to Spain on a smaller replacement vessel. The Romantic painter Caspar David Friedrich produced a number of metaphorical images of loss on his canvases depicting sailing ships foundering in the polar sea, providing a moral commentary on the phenomenon, which he observed from an objective distance. And in his study *Shipwreck with Spectator*, the German philosopher and intellectual historian Hans Blumenberg has advanced the view that 'there is a frivolous, if not blasphemous, moment inherent in all human seafaring, on a par with an offense against the invulnerability of the earth, the law of *terra inviolata*'.[6]

The myth of the *Titanic* is already enshrined in the liner's oracular name, for Titanism is regarded as immoderate pride: in Greek myth the Titans – descendants of Uranus – rose up against Zeus, who punished them by casting them down into the abyss, which was known as Tartarus. When the *Titanic* sank, the *Baptist Courier* of South Carolina was convinced that 'the disaster is a judgment of God'.[7]

But it was only because of the particular conditions that obtained in 1912 that the loss of the *Titanic* became a global media event. Even before the survivors had reached the safe haven of New York and before the first eyewitness reports had been filed, there were already rumours circulating about the causes of the catastrophe, resulting in what was effectively a live commentary manipulating the emotions of a collective public all over the world. Without the use of modern wireless telegraphy, without the rapid dissemination of images and sounds immediately after the disaster and without the new telephone networks and aftereffects in and through the medium of the cinema, including James Cameron's epic film, it is highly unlikely that there would have been a *Titanic* myth. And the myth lived on not just in the cinema but also as great literature, notably in the novel by the Norwegian writer Erik Fosnes Hansen, *Psalm at*

Journey's End, and in Hans Magnus Enzensberger's epic poem, *The Sinking of the 'Titanic'*.

It was the Germans who showed themselves to be particularly affected by the disaster in the North Atlantic. Such was their own sense of national disorientation that the image of a foundering 'ship of state' became a prophetic metaphor, allowing observers to compare the trajectory of the Kaiserreich with the fatal final journey of the *Titanic*. In this context, an anecdote attributed to the Prussian diplomat Philipp zu Eulenburg seems especially telling. He was recalling the Kaiser's visit to Scandinavia: 'Well, I asked the pilot where the Kaiser was going. – North? South? East? West? – "No," he said, drawling his words: "I've no particular direction in mind".'[8] Exactly the same mood is found in Oswald Spengler's book *The Decline of the West* (*Der Untergang des Abendlandes*), the first part of which appeared in the immediate aftermath of the First World War, quickly becoming a bestseller. Even though Spengler always refused to draw a parallel between his prophecy of doom and the sinking (in German, *Untergang*) of the ocean liner, it is surely no accident that he had already settled on the title of his book in 1912. A historian and a philosopher by training, he was convinced that the modern world was facing a process of decline similar to the one that had affected classical antiquity. By choosing a title that recalled the fate of the *Titanic*, he gave graphic expression to the increasingly apocalyptic mood of the age, when Europe's picture of the world was being shaken to its very foundations. The stage of decline reached by classical western structures, Spengler argued, was identical to the destructive nucleus of 'civilization'. 'Civilization', he went on, was at odds with 'culture', a discrepancy that was not only chronological but also topographical, inasmuch as it marked a fault line that ran between Germany and the West.

But it was only with the outbreak of the First World War that this antinomy was reduced to a purely functional role. Two years earlier, the loss of the *Titanic* could still be felt as the great tragic manifestation of a cultural loss that was bound to elicit pity and self-pity in Germany and elsewhere, whereas the sinking of the *Lusitania* in 1915 could be celebrated as what Thomas Mann termed 'the destruction of that impudent symbol of English mastery of the sea and of a still comfortable civilization'.[9] Recent research by a Swiss team of social scientists has shown that the social backgrounds and norms were different in the two disasters: on the *Titanic* a higher than average percentage of first-class passengers survived, whereas on the *Lusitania* fewer third-class passengers died than those in first class, at least in percentage terms. The fact that in spite of the adverse conditions, including the ship's rapid disappearance beneath the waves, third-class passengers from the *Lusitania* were able to gain access to the liner's lifeboats was due not only to their sharper elbows but also to the circumstance that, in general, conditions on deck were more democratic and less class-bound than had been the case with the *Titanic*, where traditional social hierarchies had been preserved quite literally to the end, even the ship's orchestra famously having to play till the vessel went down. It was a symbolic social order that went down with the *Titanic* and one for which the majority of Germans, too, were inclined to mourn.

In the wake of the disaster, the Germans pinned their hopes on a new 'German *Titanic*'. At the time that the White Star Line was planning its Olympic class of liners, the general director of HAPAG, Albert Ballin, was still attempting to reach an international agreement to limit the cut-throat competition between the different shipping companies on the North Atlantic routes. But when the pressure of competition between the various economic interests on the part of the major powers proved to be too great, HAPAG sought to beat the English at their own game and build a new fleet of liners of its own.

On 23 May 1912, only weeks after the *Titanic* had been lost, the *Imperator* – the first of the Imperator class of ships – was launched from the Vulcan Shipyards in Hamburg. Her sister ships, the *Vaterland* and the *Bismarck*, were built at the Blohm & Voss Shipyards and followed in 1913 and 1914 respectively, each of them bigger than her predecessor. But even the *Imperator* was a superliner, its tonnage of 52,117 tons 6,000 more than that of the *Titanic*. She also had a hitherto unprecedented capacity, with room for 4,300 passengers and a crew of 1,200.

As the Swiss journalist Karl Friedrich Kunz observed with some incredulity in 1913, such a 'huge monster' had 'ceased to be a ship at all' but was 'a floating city, an impregnable bulwark, a leviathan for which we have no word in any of our existing languages'.[10]

The new HAPAG liner was originally to have been called the *Europa*, for, according to the company's publicity, there was 'nothing more peaceful than the journey of a merchant vessel from one part of the world to another'. But the company was forced to concede that 'with its tremendous size, its steam-driven power and its steel armour', the ship was 'too strong, too mighty and too threatening for it not also to appear like a military transport'. Yet, as the publicity material sought to water down the implied threat, it was a 'warship directed not against people but against the elemental ocean'.[11] This remarkable contradiction was entirely typical of Wilhelmine propaganda at this time, with its bewildering mixture of assurances that the country wanted only peace and its simultaneous sabre-rattling. The name of the vessel was proposed by the Kaiser himself – he was fond of being described as Imperator Rex – and it was Wilhelm, too, who demanded that the bow of the ship be adorned with an aggressive symbol in the form of an imperial eagle cast from bronze, its beak wide open and its wings fully extended to a width of over 50 feet (16 metres). On the eagle's head was set the Kaiser's crown, while its powerful talons clasped a globe bearing the words 'My field is the world'. This painfully ostentatious figurehead was a reflection of the liner's interior, whose showy extravagance, lacking in style, was mocked by contemporaries as 'Potsdam Rococo'.

In the event, neither the 'German *Titanic*' nor her two sister ships enjoyed a career as glorious or as dramatic as her martial insignia implied. The *Imperator* began her final voyage under a German flag on 8 July 1914 but was then laid up in the port of Hamburg following the outbreak of the First World War. After the war the Kaiser's favourite liner was acquired by Cunard and became known as the *Berengaria*. According to the reminiscences of Arthur Henry Rostron, who as captain of the *Carpathia* was responsible for rescuing seven hundred of the *Titanic*'s passengers and who later became the commodore of the Cunard fleet, memories of the vessel's German past faded very quickly; writing enthusiastically about the significance of the *Mauritania* and *Lusitania*, each of which is treated to a separate chapter, he mentions the *Berengaria* in only a single phrase, describing her merely as a 'comfortable' vessel.[12]

The other two HAPAG liners were likewise quickly forgotten. The *Vaterland* was in New York when the First World War broke out. Impounded by the United States, she was later renamed the *Leviathan*. For her part, the *Bismarck* was completed only after the war and made her maiden voyage in 1922 as the *Majestic* as part of the White Star Line's fleet. Otherwise, the great civilian liners of the HAPAG fleet had only one – limited – use after the war: all of the ships belonging to the country's naval fleet were scuttled on German orders, their only value being as scrap metal.

CHAPTER 2

Modern Vikings?

The 'risk fleet'

The roots of the First World War lay in old territorial, social, economic and religious conflicts between the various European states. Since the 1870s Europe had witnessed increasing militarization, but the fact that German industry's markets were almost all in foreign hands was seen as a source of national shame, leading Wilhelm II to demand more colonies in order to guarantee a 'place in the sun' for the German Reich. At the same time it was clear that a major colonial power would also require a powerful navy. Although Germany traditionally had a large army, its fleet was insignificant in comparison. In spite of its extended coastline along the shores of the Baltic, Brandenburg-Prussia had limited itself to using the army to maintain its grip on a region marked by internal divisions.

The desire to conquer the sea brought to German politics a new and nationalist element that was profoundly un-Prussian. The Kaiser declared himself the nation's 'first sea lord' and turned the navy into a self-governing body. Admiral Alfred von Tirpitz, who was appointed secretary of state at the Imperial Naval Department in 1897, was keen to build up the country's battle fleet. Even the draft bill of 1900 made it clear that naval rearmament was directed first and foremost at Great Britain: the fleet, it was argued, must be big enough to ensure that 'any war fought against our most powerful maritime foe must be associated with such threats that that country's position of power is called into question'. Tirpitz invented the term 'risk fleet' for this aggressive policy: in other words, a fleet that would deter potential aggressors. Tirpitz was a successful propagandist and ideologue and thanks to the Kaiser's support he was able to influence public opinion – parliamentarians, academics, diplomats and journalists – to lasting effect. It was hoped that Germany's maritime policy would find broad support among the population at large and help to stabilize the monarchy. Germany's business leaders, notably shipbuilders, steel producers and shipyard suppliers, all reacted enthusiastically to the promise of more jobs. The middle classes, too, supported the government's new policy and on public holidays dressed their children in sailor suits.

One of the few men to question this policy was the head of HAPAG, Albert Ballin, who argued that an agreement with Britain was more important for safeguarding shipping and world trade than building a battle fleet. But Tirpitz continued to pursue his policy of ostensible deterrence: if the British Empire were to be afraid of a modern German fleet, it would not dare to engage in war. The truth of the matter is that he was hoping for a decisive naval battle in the North Sea that could be won by the new German battleships within the shortest possible time 'with the ultimate in fighting strength and steadfastness'.

Meanwhile the Royal Navy was also rearming. For centuries it had been regarded as the most effective in the world and in 1904 was placed under the control of Sir John Arbuthnot Fisher as First Sea Lord. His motto was 'ruthless, relentless, remorseless'. In 1911 Winston Churchill took over as First Lord of the Admiralty, by which time the Royal Navy was twice the size of the German fleet. Unlike Tirpitz, Churchill was well aware that in naval warfare it is not a single battle that is decisive but the ability to safeguard one's own long-term strategic goals and to mount an effective blockade in order to keep foreign powers at bay. The British Navy had no need to fight the battle that Tirpitz was hoping for but could build up its lines of blockade far from the German coast and do so, moreover, without incurring any risk. While the Royal Navy's grand fleet was achieving this goal in the First World War, the German ocean-going fleet was barely used at all but rusted away while lying at anchor.

Only weeks after the outbreak of war, a battle did in fact take place that may be seen as a symbolic substitute for the great encounter envisaged by Tirpitz. This was the 'duel' between two former passenger liners, the *Carmania* of the Cunard Line and the *Cap Trafalgar* of the Hamburg South American Line. Both ships had been converted into auxiliary cruisers and met off the coast of Trinidad on 14 September 1914, when they decided to engage in hostilities. The Germans opened fire, initially concentrating on the bridge of the *Carmania*, while the British vessel aimed at the *Cap Trafalgar*'s waterline. The opening skirmishes resembled nothing so much as a scene from an operetta: the British troops were wearing pith helmets and had erected an awning to protect them from the sun, while their gunners were served chilled drinks on silver trays. But it was not long before fires broke out on both vessels, posing a serious danger. The *Carmania*'s steering, engine-room telegraph, masts and lifeboats were all damaged in the fire, while the damage to the bulkheads on the *Cap Trafalgar*, which had been hit below her waterline, eventually caused her to sink, albeit not before her crew of 279 had been rescued and transferred to a supply ship. Her captain and another fifty marines lost their lives in the encounter. There were nine deaths and many more injuries on board the *Carmania*, but in spite of the damage that she had sustained, she was able to continue on her journey with flying colours. Not even further minor skirmishes and pre-emptive strikes by other German battleships such as those that took place in the vicinity of the Dogger Bank in January 1915 were able to provoke the decisive battle desired by Tirpitz. The Royal Navy's bases remained out of the German Navy's reach, and the naval blockade became increasingly effective.

It was only when the black, white and red ensign of the German Empire had all but disappeared from the oceans of the world that the Germans discovered a new 'wonder weapon' in the form of the U-boat or submarine. When war broke out, the U-boat was relatively untried as a military weapon, neither the German nor the British navy having taken it particularly seriously – the Admiralty even dismissed it as 'un-English'. Initially the Germans had only twenty-one U-boats at their disposal, all of them intended to support their fleet in coastal waters close to home. But when the *U-9* under its commander Otto Weddingen succeeded in sinking no fewer than three British cruisers within an hour to the north of the Hook of Holland on 22 September 1914, the navy rethought its policy. The Kaiser, too, was impressed and for the first time inspected the hitherto neglected weapon at Kiel, thereby granting military and social recognition to the little band of U-boat warriors.

In general the German Navy was no longer in thrall to Prussian traditions, with the result that the sons of middle-class Germans were now able to enjoy a career in the navy and bring the modern world of engineering to the programme for the pan-German fleet. For Oswald Spengler, the power of the engineer represented the replacement of abstract philosophy by the power of actual machines: 'I can only hope,' he appealed to young Germans everywhere, 'that men of the new generation may be moved by this book to devote themselves to technics instead of lyrics, the sea instead of the paint-brush, and politics instead of epistemology. Better they could not do.'[1] Heinrich Mann, conversely, was quick to warn of the dangers of a cultic reverence of 'military machines' and of the middle class's new and 'soulless' attitude to violence.[2] It was not long before even the sailors on the new warships had lost their initial enthusiasm for the war: frustrated by the long and futile wait for the decisive battle that they had been promised, they began to rebel against the senseless exercises to which they were subjected and the privileges of their superiors. Surviving letters and diaries reflect the growing lack of trust between officers and marines. The situation was completely different in the U-boats, torpedo boats and minesweepers that were in constant use. Here officers and their crews were exposed to the same pressures and risks and as a result they formed a much more close-knit community.

The submarines were cramped, the air inside them stuffy and their crews had to contend not only with enemy action but also with the forces of nature. In northern waters in winter the temperature inside the submarine sank to 4°C and was bearable only with special leather clothing and woollen underwear. In summer or when the submarines were deployed in the Mediterranean, the heat and foul air were equally disagreeable. Since the electric motors had only limited capacity, the submarines generally stayed on the surface, allowing them to use their petrol-driven motors and recharge their batteries. (Petroleum was later replaced by diesel fuel.) The stench of diesel, oil, leftover food, sweat and other human smells not only spread throughout the whole ship but clung to the clothes of the entire crew. On longer voyages, their olfactory senses would gradually become dulled, so that hygiene ceased to be a pressing concern. If external danger meant that a submarine was unable to surface for any length of time, the build-up of carbon dioxide and other harmful gases would eventually cause breathing difficulties for the crew. And whenever the batteries were discharged, not only was inflammable hydrogen released, there was also the danger that the mixture of sulphuric acid and salt water would produce lethal chlorine gas. In short, every submarine voyage was an unpleasant and potentially life-threatening exercise, even without the threat of enemy action.

Anyone who volunteered to serve on a submarine must already have been fired by fanaticism and by a marked desire to go to war. It was this will that the economist Werner Sombart glorified in his 1915 pamphlet *Shopkeepers and Heroes* and to which a number of U-boat captains lent an aura of mystery in writing about their 'Viking adventures', writings that served as self-propaganda. Among those who produced this kind of promotional material, either as self-appointed apologists or as writers commissioned to contribute to the debate, were Max Valentiner, Georg Günther von Forstner and Werner Fürbringer, while the Imperial Navy even employed its own official war artist, Claus Bergen, who had previously made a name for himself illustrating the writings of the German author Karl May. He became known chiefly for his illustrations of the Battle of Jutland but he also took part in a number of U-boat exercises, which he later captured on canvas. It was inevitable that the *Lusitania* disaster would also provide him with material for his work. He spoke to crew members of the *U-20* and within weeks of the disaster he had already completed his painting *The Sinking of the 'Lusitania'*. After that, the depiction of U-boat captains as salty heroes became a favourite theme among artists of the period.

Many of Max Valentiner's texts were garishly crude and simplistic:

> The first impression that the captains of merchant vessels formed of us was certainly a terrifying one. The creatures that rose up from the depths of the sea and fired at them with their torpedoes seemed not to be human at all but barbarians from a strange primeval age. We looked as if we had painted ourselves like North American Indians before going on the war-path. But this was in fact involuntary, for the air in the U-boat was permanently thick with oil, which, reddish yellow in colour, settled on our skin. There were times when we were unable to wash for weeks on end. Even the landlubber knows that it is impossible to wash in seawater, and although we had freshwater on board, this was so precious that we were not even allowed to drink it. Instead, we drank cognac and whisky. The ships that we commandeered had enough brandy on board. We needed our freshwater to cool our engines. And so we rose up from the depths of the sea, red-faced like primitive barbarians, our faces framed by prickly stubble. The whites of our eyes stood out with startling clarity, with the result that we involuntarily recalled a scene from Tacitus: Tacitus, it will be remembered, reports that many of the Germanic tribes had the ability to intimidate their enemies merely by looking at them. We had been endowed with this appearance by the armouries of war even without our knowing it.

According to Valentiner, it 'went without saying' that right from the start of the war the crews of German U-boats would be 'hand-picked', and he himself had 'chosen only the jewels from this hand-picked material'.[3]

These hand-picked U-boat Vikings played no part in the naval mutinies of October and November 1918. All of them refused to fly the red flag and regarded Germany's defeat and the November Revolution as a 'twofold shame'. Many joined the counterrevolutionary Freikorps organizations and continued their careers under National Socialism and during the Second World War. This was especially true of Admiral Karl Dönitz, whom Hitler appointed his successor in April 1945 under the terms of his last will and testament. Dönitz, too, had volunteered to work on a submarine in 1916 and by the time he had completed his first tours of duty on the *U-39*, the then twenty-five-year-old was being described as a 'fresh and energetic officer' and was promoted to the rank of lieutenant. While deployed in the Mediterranean in October 1918, Dönitz was captured by the British. He remained loyal to the navy throughout the years of the Weimar Republic, when he was promoted to the rank of staff officer. He continued his career during the Second World War as rear admiral and commander-in-chief of the country's fleet of submarines, devising a new form of attack involving 'wolfpacks', whereby several submarines would launch a joint attack on shipping. As commander-in-chief of the navy he was responsible for giving orders for his men to hold out following the lost Battle of the Atlantic. Even during the Nuremberg Trials, when he was accused of 'sinking enemy merchant vessels without any prior warning', he was pleased to play the part of an unquestioningly loyal National Socialist.

In 1917, when Dönitz was officer of the watch on the *U-39*, a fellow crew member was Martin Niemöller, who later studied theology and became a leading pacifist. In the February of that year, when he was navigator on the submarine, Niemöller was involved in the sinking of two troopships, the French *Amiral Magon* and the Italian *Minas*, with the loss of over 1,000 lives. In his book *From U-Boat to Pulpit*, which was first published in 1934, he admitted that he had felt uncomfortable sabotaging the rescue of so many helpless men. His book also documents the difficulty that even he had in breaking free from his perception of himself as an elite combatant and from the National Conservative ideology in which he had grown up. On the outbreak of the Second World War, by which time he was already a prisoner in the Ravensbrück concentration camp, he wanted to offer Hitler his services as a U-boat commander, but the Führer turned down his request.

Hitler's enigmatic defence chief, Wilhelm Canaris, likewise began his career as an unscrupulous U-boat officer in the First World War. Canaris hailed from a family of entrepreneurs and on leaving school joined the Imperial Navy as a sea cadet. He was eighteen at the time. After training on a cruiser and various torpedo ships, he received his first secret-service commissions in the Mediterranean and Latin America. In 1915 he began to build up a supply organization for the German U-boats operating in the Mediterranean and under the code name of Reed Rosas established a network of agents working in naval intelligence in Spanish coastal towns. The following year he asked to be transferred to active submarine duty and as the commander of the *U-34* and *UB-128* was responsible for sinking numerous British and French merchant vessels.

Canaris was never as unimpeachable as he was made out to be in the 1954 German biopic, in which he was played by the actor Otto Eduard Hasse, and this is also true of his activities in the marine brigade's Freikorps following the November Revolution and as adjutant to the Weimar Republic's defence minister, Gustav Noske. Particularly shameful was his involvement in the plot to murder the Spartacist leaders Rosa Luxemburg and Karl Liebknecht. From the outset he was sympathetic to the cause of National Socialism and it was no surprise when he was appointed defence chief in the Wehrmacht's High Command in 1935. Although the rivalry between the Defence Ministry and the SS was one of the more spectacular conflicts in the Third Reich's Byzantine power structure, Canaris was never a member of the resistance to Hitler. In February 1944 the Defence Ministry was placed under the control of the Reich Main Security Office and on 9 April 1945 Canaris was executed at the Flossenbürg concentration camp for his alleged links to those men and women who had tried to assassinate Hitler on 20 July 1944.

A number of the U-boat 'heroes' of the First World War such as Otto Steinbrinck and Max Valentiner, both of whom received Pour le Mérite awards, not only continued their careers after 1933 in National Socialist military organizations but also gained considerable influence as leading industrialists. Steinbrinck, who was the most successful of the Flanders commanders, captaining five different U-boats between 1914 and 1918, joined not only the National Socialist German Workers' Party but also the SS in May 1933. Within two years he had risen to the rank of SS Oberführer (senior leader) and had persuaded one of his friends, the leading industrialist Friedrich Flick, to join his Circle of Friends of SS Leaders. From April 1938 he held the titles of Wehrwirtschaftsführer (the designation of industrialists important to Germany's armaments industry) and general plenipotentiary for the Flick conglomerate. In 1939 he was appointed SS brigade leader and was re-enlisted as the captain of a frigate, although his departure from Flick certainly did not mean that he abandoned his positions of economic power. From 1940 to 1945 he worked as a trustee of Thyssen, as a member of the supervisory body of United Steelworks, as general plenipotentiary for the steel industry in Luxembourg, Belgium and France, as a director of the Reich Coal Board and, shortly before the end of the war, as intermediary between the Ruhr industrial concerns and Army Group B under General Field Marshal Walter Model. In December 1947, in the Nuremberg Flick Trial, the Allies sentenced the National Socialists' jack-of-all-trades to five years' imprisonment. He died in prison, suffering a fatal heart attack in 1949.

Steinbrinck's old U-boat comrade, Max Valentiner, also died in 1949. A highly decorated veteran of the First World

War, he, too, pursued a brilliant dual career, not only holding a leading position in the Naval Department at the Reich Ministry of Defence but also acquiring a vast personal fortune as a shipping magnate and factory owner. He suffered from progressive pulmonary disease incurred by inhaling poisonous engine fumes during his time as a U-boat commander. Between the autumn of 1917 and the spring of 1918 he established a record for remaining at sea for a total of 139 days, during which time he sank 150 vessels, a feat that quickly became the stuff of legend. Even before he took command of the large new submarine cruiser, the *U-157*, he had additionally made a name for himself as the author of a series of autobiographical adventures: in 1917 Ullstein published his first book, *300,000 Tons Sunk! My U-Boat Missions*, the foreword of which contains the boastful claim that 'When I sat down to write these lines, the *U-38* alone had sunk ships with a total tonnage of around 300,000 tons'.[4]

In fact, Valentiner did not write the book himself but had help from a ghost-writer by the name of Reinhard Roehle, a former HAPAG purser who had turned his hand to travel writing. According to his contract with Ullstein, Roehle was required to write down Valentiner's experiences on the basis of the submarine's logbooks. Valentiner himself was guaranteed a fee of 20,000 marks, while Roehle was to receive 4,000. Since the contract was signed before the end of his deployment on the *U-38*, the logs relating to his final acts of piracy were intended in the first instance to further his aspirations as a writer, with the result that their tone becomes correspondingly euphemistic and cynical, notably in his account of the sinking of a French passenger liner that was evidently being used as a troopship:

> Once we are closer, we have a good view of the liner. It is a troopship. Its decks are filled with mostly coloured soldiers, Turks and Moroccans. Each is wearing a red fez. But what is the matter with these people? Why do they show no sign of launching their lifeboats? Their captain can surely not think that I would allow a troopship to escape unscathed. We have already paralysed her. Why, in God's name, does he not lower the lifeboats and bring his men to safety? I am not just a sailor but also a soldier. We are at war. I give orders to shoot. A torpedo is fired, and the men over there see it coming. They panic, each of them falling over the other, resulting in pandemonium. Ruthlessly they trample each other underfoot, but the officers are the least willing to evacuate the area where my torpedo will strike. It hits the vessel amidships. The men now throw themselves into the lifeboats and are lowered into the water at incredible speed. Some of the boats are so overloaded that their ropes break and their occupants are thrown into the water. Burying their occupants beneath them, the boats hit the water and break into a thousand pieces. But most of the soldiers simply do not wait until the boats have been lowered, preferring to leap from the deck head first and to attempt to reach the Moroccan coast by swimming. By the time that the liner capsizes ten minutes

> later, the decks are completely empty. The crippled ship disappears beneath the waves at lightning speed.[5]

Hundreds of shipwrecked soldiers were abandoned to their fate for the captain had already set his sights on another objective: 'The terrible scenes taking place on board the troopship were still unfolding before us when we sighted a liner that was heading to France.' This time, the reader learns, the encounter took place according to the rules of engagement. On this occasion there were no undisciplined troops on board but only a cargo of grain. 'We surface and fire a warning shot. The steamer immediately surrenders. The boats are let down in an orderly manner. We blast the ship out of the water.'[6]

Even after the war Valentiner's book continued to be reprinted, each time with a high print-run. In 1934, for example, Ullstein republished it under the title *U-38: Viking Voyages of a German U-Boat*, and even as recently as 2002 it reappeared practically unchanged, this time advertised as a novel with the title *Mortal Danger Above Us: The U-38 on Deployment*. The myth of the U-boat that had been created during the First World War drew on existential human experiences of technology, fear and aggression, images of which continue to fascinate us today even though we may never have experienced war for ourselves. These images represent an eerie, mortal danger from the depths of the ocean, but they also capture a sense of courage, camaraderie and the triumph of the weak over the strong. According to Günther Rohrbach, the producer of the hugely successful

German television mini-series *Das Boot*, 'The U-boat is not just a cage in which people are trapped, it is also a dangerous animal.'[7]

The enthusiasm and admiration triggered by the deployment of German U-boats in the First World War were encouraged in no small way by the emphasis placed by propagandists on their function as a sophisticated all-purpose weapon. Some 320 German U-boats were deployed in that conflict, carrying out 3,240 missions, in the course of which 6,000 civilian vessels and more than 100 larger warships were sunk. The total number of lives lost is not known, but in the course of September and October 1914 alone more than 2,000 British mariners perished as a result of the actions of a single German submarine, the *U-9*. Its commander, Otto Weddingen, was the first German naval officer to receive the order Pour le Mérite. He himself died only a few months later when his boat was rammed by a British battleship off the Scottish coast, sinking with all hands. A total of 187 German U-boats and more than 5,000 crew members were lost in the course of the war.

'We're sailing off to Eng-e-land'

U-boats were deployed not only in the North Sea and Atlantic but also in the Mediterranean, where they were of particular significance. Max Valentiner, for example, attacked Italian vessels in the Adriatic even before Italy was officially at war with Germany. Later, while still in command of the *U-38*, he hoisted the Austro-Hungarian flag in a deliberate attempt to confuse the Italian cruise ship, the *Ancona*, which he then proceeded to sink. It was also German U-boats that established links with the Arab rebels in Tripoli, transported sensitive material to North Africa and supplied the bullets and fuses needed to defend the Dardanelles. They protected the offshore flank during the Turkish advance on the Suez Canal, defended the Bulgarian coast and prevented the Russians from transporting materials and munitions through the White Sea.

But their principal enemy was Great Britain, a point underscored by a piece of propaganda dating from 1915:

> In its proud unapproachability and in the utter certainty of its everlasting power, England never imagined in its wildest dreams that German U-boats would destroy English warships, sink English merchantmen, force English shipping to reduce its activities, raise wage costs, freight costs and insurance premiums, foment strikes, increase the price of foodstuffs and throw the whole of English trade into a state of upheaval and confusion, but this is precisely what German U-boats have done, ensuring that England's standing as the absolute ruler of the waves has begun to decline in not inconsiderable ways.[8]

This propaganda text makes no mention of a problem associated with the unscrupulous sinking of merchantmen demanded by sections of the German naval command.

According to the rules of international law, enemy trading vessels first had to be searched, at which point their cargo could be seized and the vessel towed into port and impounded. Sinking the vessel was only a last resort once the safety of the crew could be guaranteed. But such a course of action was scarcely practicable in the case of U-boats, which lacked the space to seize the cargo and rescue the crews of enemy vessels.[9] It also has to be said that in imposing their naval blockade the British did not always abide by the rules of international law: they had declared practically the whole of the North Sea a war zone and laid mines in international waters, so that not even neutral shipping could pass through them without being checked and piloted.

The German Admiralty justified its demands for an all-out U-boat war by pointing to Britain's violations of international law. The German chancellor, Theobald von Bethmann Hollweg, was under no illusions as to the political consequences of such a course of action and tried to restrain Tirpitz and his minions, but the protests of the admirals and the pressure of public opinion continued to grow, and on 4 February 1915 the German government finally declared the waters around Great Britain a war zone. After 18 February every enemy trading vessel could be sunk 'without its always being possible to avert the danger to its crew and passengers'. Nor could the government 'prevent neutral ships from being hit in attacks aimed at enemy vessels'.

Although the German U-boat command was assured that they would be covered in the event of torpedo attacks on vessels 'mistakenly' thought to be enemy ships, the commanders themselves felt that this provision was insufficiently radical. 'If it had been left to us U-boat captains,' wrote Max Valentiner,

> we would have encircled England and sunk everything that came into our line of fire. We could have continued our business at night using torpedoes, and England would certainly not have felt comfortable for very long in our grip and would have had to sue for peace. But it wasn't left to us. The government ordered us to conduct a thorough search of every steamship that we stopped. Only when we were completely certain that the neutral flag of the steamship was a false one or that the steamship had contraband on board or was being used by the Allies were we allowed to sink it. As a result of this approach we inevitably had to allow more vessels to go on their way than we were able to sink. [. . .] Our U-boats could have sunk one million tons a day during the early days of the war. If we had been able to fire on every vessel without first having to search it, every U-boat could have destroyed thirty vessels a day with a total tonnage of 100,000 tons without any extra effort.[10]

Valentiner was dissatisfied with his work in the North Sea, finding it too 'tedious' and applying instead for a new posting in the Mediterranean, which he justified with an appeal to Goethe's *Iphigenia on Tauris*: 'It is entirely possible that at least once in his life every German is seized by this longing for the south, this hope on the part of the Northerner that repeatedly proves to be an illusion, namely, that he may come closer to finding the meaning of life in the blazing heat of the sun and beneath the blue of the sky.' He also drew on his knowledge of art history in selecting a new camouflage colour for these southern climes:

> The North Sea is grey, and so the U-boats were painted grey, giving us good protection. But we are steaming towards the Aegean. Böcklin painted the Aegean. I knew Böcklin and so I was able to take the liberty of addressing my mentor on the question of painting U-boats. [. . .] I had the *U-38* painted bright blue like the sea in Böcklin's painting *In the Play of the Waves*. The colour was wonderful, and in the Mediterranean we were impeccably protected by being painted a deep blue colour.[11]

In the Mediterranean the greatest risk was posed by piracy and hijacking, and so Valentiner sought to rearm his submarine accordingly, but his request to the navy to remove the bulkheads that had been installed as a safety measure and 'to use the extra capacity to carry more munitions' was turned down. Although he had to comply with this decision, he was unwilling to forgo an additional second gun and at his own expense he installed a 'semi-automatic speed-loader'.[12] Thus equipped, Valentiner became one of the most unscrupulous hunters in the Mediterranean, confirming his international reputation as a war criminal when he sank the Italian passenger liner *Ancona* on 8 November 1915 and torpedoed the British passenger liner *Persia* without any preliminary warning on 30 December. The combined death toll was 551.

After the war Valentiner was accused by the victorious powers of France, Great Britain and Italy of 'the cruel and inhuman treatment of his fellow human beings'. The French described his war crimes as acts of 'bestialité extraordinaire'. In his *Viking Tales* he himself wrote that

> The English and especially the French believed that U-boat commanders were consumed by great hatred and inner fury when carrying out their work of destruction, but this view is completely inaccurate. Of course, there were a handful of exceptions, but most captains behaved with absolute objectivity. Without a hint of hatred, they tried to carry out their terrible task in as humane a way as possible. Everyone who truly knows the German national character will confirm my view on this matter.[13]

The final sentence was removed from the 2002 edition of Valentiner's book.

In the event, Valentiner escaped sentence. He fled to Berlin at the end of the war, when his name was removed from the list of naval officers and he was given a new identity as Karl Schmidt. Once the Treaty of Versailles had come into force, he was absolved of all crimes and promoted to the rank of lieutenant commander. It was in this role that Hitler's navy reactivated him in 1934.

The Imperial German Navy kept a detailed record of the vessels sunk by its U-boats, but it was not interested in the number of victims, only in the tonnage of the vessels sunk. According to official figures, civilian ships weighing a total of 12 million tons were sunk in the course of the war, while the figure for warships reached only a fraction of that number. All of these figures were based in part on estimates and often varied wildly, although there was no question as to who was the most 'successful' hunter: the captain of the *U-35*, Lothar von Arnauld de la Perière, who topped the list with the proud total of more than 500,000 gross register tons. His closest rival was Valentiner. For both men, the Mediterranean was the most popular and most profitable hunting ground, where easy prey was to be found.

Other commanders, such as Walther Schwieger of the *U-20*, Erich von Rosenberg-Gruszcynski of the *U-30* and Bernhard Wegener of the *U-27*, were forced to continue to defy the enemy in the North Sea and Atlantic, where the principal concern was breaking the British blockade and disrupting supplies to the British Isles. In view of the insidious English submarine traps and the increasing frequency with which German U-boats were rammed by merchant vessels, Schwieger and his comrades were delighted when Gustav Bachmann, chief of staff at the Admiralty, ordered his crews to be less scrupulous when attacking enemy vessels. According to his guidelines of 13 February 1915, it was 'in the military interest to make sure that the U-boat war is as effective as possible. It is not appropriate to shy away from destroying passenger liners that clearly belong to enemy nations. Rather, it is their destruction that will leave behind the greatest impression.'[14] The *Lusitania* could therefore be fired on. The chief of staff of the German Admiralty having personally signed her death warrant, the sentence was carried out only three months later by the commander of the *U-20*, Lieutenant Commander Walther Schwieger.

Who was this man, who with a single torpedo was to trigger a disaster and influence world opinion? We know little about him, not least because unlike his friend Max Valentiner, he was never motivated by an exaggerated love of self-promotion. His logbooks are brief and to the point and he evidently played no part in drafting propaganda. He was born in Berlin in 1885, his well-respected family having a long tradition of providing the country with architects, surveyors and engineers. The navy marked a new departure for the family, but for Walther Schwieger it opened up the way to a promising career. He began as a cadet in 1903 and was appointed lieutenant commander on the outbreak of the First World War. He received his first U-boat command in 1912 and became commander of the *U-20* on 16 December 1914, and between then and his death in a minefield in the North Sea on 5 September 1917 he sank not only the *Lusitania* but another forty-eight ships with a total weight of 184,000 gross register tons, making him the sixth most successful captain in the navy's inglorious rankings.

His thirtieth birthday, on 7 April 1915, found him returning to his home port of Emden after another successful mission. In the course of the on-board celebrations, his gramophone, which was normally used for classical light music, played the popular 'Sailors' Song' by Hermann Löns with its chorus 'We're sailing off to Eng-e-land', while the raucous crew joined in. Even on Christmas Eve that year there were celebrations on board the *U-20*, for all that the boat was on patrol. But in the depths of the North Sea, the party bore no resemblance to the scenes of fraternization that took place in the trenches at Verdun and on the battlefields of Flanders on and after 24 December 1914. There the German soldiers, exhausted by the materiel battles, ignored their officers and, laying aside their weapons, lit candles decorated with pine needles. And when carols such as *Silent Night* were heard rising from the German trenches, their 'enemies' applauded and emerged into no-man's-land to embrace their French and British foes. No such shows of Christian fraternization took place in the North Sea. Candles could not be lit for reasons of safety, but there was plenty of tinned meat and tea laced with rum, accompanied by a speech from the boat's commander designed to boost morale.

Outwardly, too, Schwieger was a typical Viking: fair-haired, tall and broad-shouldered. His crew held him in high regard, and he could trust them. Among his qualities were ambition, nerves of steel, and boldness. Even before the Admiralty's instructions of 13 February 1915 his attacks had been notable for their ruthlessness. On 30 January, for example, he sank three English freighters without warning off Le Havre, and in February he tried to torpedo the hospital ship *Asturias* even though it was clearly carrying the insignia of the Red Cross. In the event, his shot missed its mark. He drew no distinction between military and civilian victims and had no time for sentimentality.

Walther Schwieger and his comrades saw themselves as modern Vikings and acted accordingly, acutely aware of the deterrent effect of such a comparison. The victims of German U-boat attacks were certainly reminded of the Norsemen who had brought fear and terror to the whole of Europe well over a thousand years earlier. Heavily armed, the Viking pirates would suddenly appear in their surprisingly manoeuvrable longships on mainland coasts and island shorelines, plundering villages and monasteries, enslaving the local population and burning down everything that they could not take with them. Following the Viking attack on the monastery at Lindisfarne, the famous Anglo-Saxon scholar Alcuin wrote to Ethelred of Northumbria to lament that 'Never before has such terror appeared in Britain.'[15] But such terror was to return with the sinking of the *Lusitania*, an act interpreted in Germany as one carried out by German 'heroes' and designed to liberate their country from the alleged hypocrisy and laziness of a nation of Anglo-Saxon shopkeepers.

CHAPTER 3

Minutes of a Disaster

By the autumn of 1914 the *Lusitania* was the last remaining large passenger liner operating on the North Atlantic route, all other similar vessels, including the *Mauretania*, having been commandeered as troopships, auxiliary cruisers or hospital ships. For the German Navy this represented a particular provocation, for while its own war fleet and its two new cruise liners, the *Imperator* and *Vaterland*, were prevented from leaving port, a large English luxury liner was regularly – and ostentatiously – crossing the Atlantic without an escort. Even after war broke out, the *Lusitania* made seventeen crossings without sustaining any harm, with the result that she was seen by the Germans – in Thomas Mann's words – as 'that impudent symbol of English mastery of the sea and of a still comfortable civilization'.[1]

For the British, she was a safe ship – her high speed and manoeuvrability appeared to rule her out as a target of torpedo attacks. And yet even in February and March 1915 three German U-boats, the *U-30*, *U-27* and *U-20*, had tried to hunt her down, their attempts thwarted only by the rivalry between their three commanders. At the end of

February the *U-27* had lain in wait for the *Lusitania* on her approach route to Liverpool, allowing smaller vessels to pass in the hope of bringing down a larger prize. According to his wartime diary, Commander Bernhard Wegener had learnt that the *Lusitania* was expected imminently in English waters and believed that in his present position he had 'a good chance' of attacking the liner.[2] But he waited in vain, for the *Lusitania* had been forewarned by the uncoordinated actions of other U-boats. She was about to enter the St George's Channel between Ireland and Wales when her captain, David Dow, received word via the ship's radio that a U-boat – the *U-20* – had torpedoed the freighter *Bengrove* close at hand and that two other merchant vessels had previously been sunk by another German submarine, the *U-30*, in the same area. Dow altered his course and reached home safely, but in the light of the dangers to which he and his ship had been exposed, he refused to accept responsibility for any further crossings. He was replaced by Captain William Thomas Turner in March 1915. It was Turner who was to take command of the vessel on her tragic final voyage.

Turner was a very different man from his predecessor: whereas the cosmopolitan Dow shone in the company of his first-class passengers, engaging in polite conversation and not shying away from taking complaints to the Cunard chairman in person, the stockily built Turner was famous, rather, for his taciturnity and brusqueness and, speaking in his broad Liverpudlian accent, is said to have described the passengers at his dinner table as 'a load of bloody monkeys who are constantly chattering'.[3] But although he may have neglected his social duties as the captain of a luxury liner, he enjoyed a fine reputation as a capable seaman. He was fifty-nine at the time in question and could look back on a distinguished career that was now drawing towards a close. He had already captained the *Lusitania* between 1908 and 1910 before taking over the *Mauretania* and establishing a new record in the race for the Blue Riband.

Turner hailed from an old seafaring family and had joined the profession at the age of eight, starting as a cabin boy on a barque, the *Grasmere*, and subsequently surviving all manner of storms and shipwrecks. He was twenty-two when he joined Cunard, although the brusqueness of his manner meant that his career advanced only slowly, with the result that it was not until 1886 that he gained his captain's licence and not until 1903, when he was forty-seven, that he was given his first command as captain of the *Aleppo*. He won respect as the captain of the *Lusitania* and *Mauretania*, so much so that when war broke out in 1914 he was given command of an auxiliary cruiser, the *Aquitania*, soon afterwards moving to the *Transylvania*, which had been converted from a passenger liner to a troopship and in which he narrowly escaped from a U-boat attack in January 1915. By the time that he retook command of the *Lusitania* in March 1915, he had gained considerable experience of war zones and blockades but appears to have underestimated the greater danger posed by German U-boats.

After replacing David Dow, Turner subjected the *Lusitania* to a thorough inspection and made a number of recommendations. Among his complaints were the crew's lack of training, the poor state of the lifeboats and the inefficiency of the turbines. Most of his demands were met: the vessel's technical shortcomings were addressed and her lifeboat facilities were improved. But no attempt was made to increase the size of her crew or improve their level of training. The reduction in the size of her crew was attributed to the difficulty in finding qualified replacements for the naval reservists who had been called up, while the decision to use only three of her four boilers was clearly a wartime expedient designed to conserve energy and save fuel – 1,600 tons of coal per crossing. Cunard accepted the implications of this reduction, for the vessel's top speed was cut from twenty-six to twenty-one knots, her cruising speed from twenty-four knots to eighteen. Cunard's supervisory board seemed certain that despite this reduction the *Lusitania* would still be able to outrun every German U-boat. In spite of this, the captain was instructed not to discuss these savings with any third parties.

The Tragedy of the *Lusitania*

These instructions were to acquire particular significance on the morning of 1 May 1915, the day on which the *Lusitania* left New York on her 202nd and final crossing. Captain Turner was having breakfast in his cabin when a steward arrived with a copy of the *New York Times*. Like every other major American newspaper, it included a 'Notice' from the Imperial German Embassy:

> Travellers intending to embark on the Atlantic voyage are reminded that a state of war exists between Germany and her allies and Great Britain and her allies; that the zone of war includes the waters adjacent to the British Isles; that, in accordance with formal notice given by the Imperial German Government, vessels flying the flag of Great Britain, or of any of her allies, are liable to destruction in those waters and that travellers sailing in the war zone on ships of Great Britain or her allies do so at their own risk.[4]

When Turner appeared on the bridge, he was able to see for himself that in addition to the bustle that was normal whenever a ship left port, there was also an exceptionally large scrum of journalists on the dockside. Automobiles and horse-drawn carriages had completely blocked off the western end of 14th Street leading to the port, and photographers were milling around among the passengers and those friends and family members who had come to wave them off. Cunard's New York general manager, Charles Sumner, had also come to Pier 54 to answer journalists' questions and reassure passengers. The Germans, he explained, had been trying for some time to disrupt his business, but until now there had been no explicit declaration that they were trying to ruin his company. And yet 'the truth remains that the *Lusitania* is the safest boat on the sea. She is too fast for any submarine. No German vessel can get her or near her.'[5] In the event, Sumner's attempt to reassure his passengers was only partly successful, a number of them remaining puzzled and perplexed by the press's unusual interest, which was directed not just at the most famous among them.

Nor was the situation helped by the fact that the multimillionaire Alfred Gwynne Vanderbilt, who was accompanied by a sizeable entourage, spoke to representatives of the press before setting foot on the gangway and confirmed the rumour that he had received an anonymous telegram with the warning: 'The *Lusitania* is doomed. Do not sail on her.' Vanderbilt appeared unruffled, dismissing the telegram as 'somebody trying to have a little fun at my expense'.[6] Most of the other passengers calmed down, too. The sight of the majestic liner, towering over the harbour wall like a skyscraper, helped to reassure them.

Preparations for the ship's departure were in full swing, with queues forming at the gangways, while items of luggage landed quickly and safely on the conveyor belts. Deep inside the vessel the stokers and engineers had spent the previous night taking the necessary steps to raise the pressure of the boilers so that by early morning dark smoke was already rising from three of its four smokestacks. In the event some hours were to pass before the *Lusitania* was finally able to depart, for a surprisingly high number of additional passengers had to be transferred to the larger vessel after the one on which they had been booked, the *Cameronia*, was requisitioned at short notice by the Royal Navy as a troopship. There were still sufficient empty cabins on the *Lusitania*, although a small number of passengers, reacting to the German warning, decided against making the crossing. It is clear from the final passenger list that the second-class accommodation was overbooked: here 601 passengers had to share cabins designed for only 400. A special offer by Cunard had led to an increase in demand.

But the lack of space was not as serious as it would otherwise have been as an unusually large number of children were travelling with their parents and were able to share their cabins. Conversely, only 290 passengers were booked into the luxurious saloon-class cabins, which were designed to accommodate 552, while the war had dramatically reduced the number of third-class passengers to 370 in cabins that could hold up to 1,200. A total of 1,264 passengers were registered, including 949 Britons (this figure also included Irish, Canadian and Australian citizens), 189 United States citizens, 71 Russians, 15 Persians and individual passengers from Argentina, Belgium, Cuba, Denmark, Finland, France, Greece, India, Italy, Mexico, the Netherlands, Norway, Spain and Switzerland. There were also 693 crew members and three stowaways, who were discovered in the ship's hold only after she had set sail.

Even while they were still on the quayside the passengers were already divided up according to class, each group having its own point of access. The eyes of the onlookers and the cameras of the photographers were directed in the main at the central gangway, which led to the luxury cabins. Here members of American and European high society celebrated their departure from New York, recalling nothing so much as a fashion show or a theatre performance. Progress was dignified, elegance and leisure the qualities held up on display. The second-class passengers, by contrast, were unassuming and well disciplined, whereas those who were booked to travel third class were in a noticeable hurry to board, the only exception a family of Russian émigrés that was being deported and leaving against their will. Once on board, most of the passengers were kept busy sorting out their luggage. Only in saloon class was this task entrusted to the passengers' servants, while the passengers themselves had nothing to do but while away their time until the ship finally departed.

One of the most striking figures on the first-class deck was the aforementioned Alfred Gwynne Vanderbilt, tall and elegantly dressed and, as always, wearing a pink carnation in the buttonhole of his dark frock coat, against which his brightly coloured trousers and white top hat stood out very clearly. It was a rig-out in which he had often been photographed at the races and one, moreover, that was well suited to his destination, a meeting of the board of directors of the International Horse Show Association in London.

Now thirty-seven, Alfred Gwynne Vanderbilt came from one of America's wealthiest families, a clan founded by the 'railroad tycoon' Cornelius Vanderbilt (1794–1877). But Alfred Gwynne seems to have inherited few of his grandfather's entrepreneurial qualities – journalists, too, were mainly interested in his numerous extramarital affairs. In his private dealings with other members of his own class, he struck observers as a highly sympathetic and even modest individual, in stark contrast to the writer and publisher

Elbert Hubbard from Illinois, who was seen standing beside him on the deck of the *Lusitania* on the morning of 1 May 1915. The author of a bestselling essay revolving around the life of a Cuban general, Calixto Garcia, *A Message to Garcia*, which was said to have sold forty million copies, he resembled his model, Mark Twain, with his Stetson hat, flamboyant cravat, corduroy trousers and knee-length overcoat. He was happy to inform the other passengers that 'Speaking from a strictly personal point of view, I would not mind if they did sink the ship. It might be a good thing for me. I would drown with her, and that's about the only way I could succeed in my ambition to get into the Hall of Fame.'[7]

Hubbard cannot for a moment have suspected that only a few days later this would indeed be his fate. Nor can he really have wanted to die with his second wife, a well-known champion of women's rights, Alice Moore. He was travelling to Europe in the hope of conducting what was to have been a sensational interview with the German Kaiser. In his periodical *The Philistine* he had already accused Wilhelm of responsibility for the German war crimes in Belgium and was keen to call him to account. The Boston literary agent and bookseller Charles Emilius Lauriat was particularly interested in marketing such an interview. Then forty years old, Lauriat had a cabin only a few doors away from the Hubbards' and was a seasoned transatlantic traveller, his voyage on the *Lusitania* marking his twenty-fifth crossing of the Atlantic. He survived the disaster and later that same year published his eyewitness account of it under the title *The Lusitania's Last Voyage*.

The distinguished theatre director Charles Frohman likewise showed little inclination to appear on deck before the *Lusitania* sailed. The son of Jewish immigrants, he was a classic example of a self-made man, having risen from paperboy to theatre impresario and stockbroker. His most successful production was his staging of J. M. Barrie's *Peter Pan*. He had booked his passage on the *Lusitania* in order to travel to Europe, as he did every year, and see for himself what was new in the theatres of the Old Continent. On this particular occasion he was interested in the performances of the French dancer, singer and actress Gaby Deslys at the Duke of York's Theatre in London. His reason for retiring to his cabin and for his subsequent reluctance to appear on deck was not only his notorious shyness but also his delicate health. Ever since an accident in 1912 he had had difficulty walking unaided. We know next to nothing about his private life. He himself never spoke about his relations with the women who travelled with him, but rumour had it that they were more than merely nurses. In the case of his voyage on the *Lusitania*, the gossipmongers were quick to note that the two actresses who were travelling with him, Rita Jolivet and Josephine Brandell, owed their Broadway careers for the most part to Frohman and that it was with touching concern that they were now devoting themselves to their benefactor's wellbeing. In fact, they were not his 'companions' but were making the crossing for various private and professional reasons of their own.

The French actress Rita Jolivet had already enjoyed her first great Hollywood success in *Fata Morgana* and was interrupting work on a new film in order to see her younger brother before he was sent off for frontline duties in France, while professional engagements on Broadway and in London meant that the English actress Josephine Brandell had for many years been commuting between America and Europe on the *Lusitania*. Among her most notable appearances were those in the review *Come Over Here* at the London Opera House (now the Peacock Theatre), which opened on 13 April 1913 and ran for 217 performances. Whereas Jolivet used the liner's late departure to join the fashion show on the first-class deck, the constitutionally nervous Josephine Brandell preferred the seclusion of the cabin of her friend Mabel Crichton, where they once again discussed the risks of the crossing.

Another female passenger who was awaiting the liner's departure with grave misgivings was Marie Depage, the wife of the head of the Belgian Red Cross. As special representative of Queen Elisabeth of the Belgians, she had been on a fundraising tour of the United States, inviting donations for medical care for the victims of the war in Europe. She was now returning to Europe with the Bostonian doctor James T. Houghton, whom she had persuaded to work with her in field hospitals on the western front. They were urgently awaited in Brussels, not least by Marie Depage's fellow worker Edith Cavell, who was running the medical school established by Antoine and Marie Depage at Ixelles.

Marie Depage was not to survive the voyage back to Europe. Only a few months later Edith Cavell, too, was to become a victim of the hostilities, when a military tribunal convened by the German occupying power found her guilty of helping wounded English and French prisoners of war to escape and sentenced her to death. She was shot 'under the articles of war' on 12 October 1915. Gottfried Benn, the Expressionist poet who was present at her execution in his official capacity as surgeon major to the German army in Brussels, commented dryly that 'She acted as a man and was punished by us as a man'.[8]

On the day of her departure Marie Depage had been filled with dark forebodings. She had been alarmed at the brutal measures used by the German occupiers in Belgium to oppress the local population. According to information that she had only recently received, the Germans were seeking to prevent the mass flight of Belgian citizens to the Netherlands by erecting an electrified fence along the border between the two countries, an expedient that was to cost many thousands of lives. Her travelling companion, James Houghton, tried in vain to dispel her doubts, but the explanation offered by the other passengers for the continuing delay to the liner's departure was hardly calculated to lift her spirits.

The delay was a particular trial for the numerous children on board the *Lusitania*. There was a kindergarten on the first-class shelter deck, with stewardesses to keep an eye on the children, but in second and third class the children's parents had to assume responsibility for the discipline of underage passengers, many of whom were fired by a spirit of adventure and curiosity. Finally, at 12.30 pm, the vessel was ready to leave, and the *Lusitania* replied to the sirens of a tug with three dull blasts on her horn before casting off. On the quayside the friends and relatives who had come to say goodbye waved hats and scarves and little flags, while the passengers on board the ship waved back. Driving a powerful bow wave before her and leaving much foam in her wake, the *Lusitania* glided down the Hudson River. The outlines of the Statue of Liberty and the Manhattan skyline gradually receded and grew more blurred, and the relief that many passengers had felt on finally getting underway was replaced by a sense of uncertainty: now there was no going back.

Early on the morning of 30 April – the day before the *Lusitania* set sail from New York – the *U-20* had left her home port of Emden on Germany's North Sea coast and had struck out in a north-westerly direction. The submarine had verbal and written orders. We do not know if the verbal instructions contained a detailed reference to the *Lusitania*'s course and schedule, although we may assume that they did. In the official, written version the order for engagement read: 'Expect large English troopships setting out from Liverpool, Bristol Channel, Dartmouth. Seek out stations on the quickest route possible round Scotland and wait there as long as supplies permit. Transport ships, merchant vessels and warships are all to be attacked.'[9]

Captain Schwieger was a cautious commander who now weighed up how, in the light of the current situation, he might deal with the rule of thumb instructing him to take 'the quickest route possible'. On earlier deployments he could have taken the shorter route through the Straits of Dover, but this stretch of the English Channel was now more dangerous thanks to the presence of the British Navy with its patrol boats, mines and submarine nets, which is why he decided to take the longer but safer route. In order to evade the British Navy he had to take his submarine round the British Isles to reach his planned hunting ground in the Irish Sea. The *U-20* therefore had a voyage of over 3,000 miles ahead of her when she passed the island of Borkum. Powered by twin diesel engines on the surface and by two battery-powered engines when the vessel was submerged, the submarine had a speed of fifteen knots on the surface but only nine when submerged. She was armed with an 88-mm deck gun and seven torpedoes filled with an explosive not unlike TNT that could be fired from four launch tubes, two of them at the bow of the submarine, the other two at her stern. The *U-20* had a crew of forty, the usual number in wartime, who had to share the damp and narrow space with the torpedo store and boat's provisions. Every deployment was exhausting and dangerous, but Schwieger knew that he could rely on his crew. In particular he trusted his pilot, Rudolf Lanz, his radio operator, Otto Rikowsky, and his torpedo officer, Rainer Weisbach.

There have been persistent rumours that the *U-20*'s crew also included 'a young electrician called Charles Voegele from Alsace' who allegedly tried to counter the order to torpedo the *Lusitania*, but there is no more basis to this report than there is to the myth of a stoker named 'Frank Tower' said to have survived not the only sinking of the

Lusitania but also the loss of the *Titanic* and the *Empress of Ireland*. Conversely, there is evidence that Schwieger had a dachshund on board his submarine as a mascot, an animal he had inherited from his predecessor Otto Dröscher and which enjoyed greater freedom than Schwieger's crew. But, as one of the captain's colleagues recalled, Schwieger

> remained on duty throughout the whole voyage and rarely had a chance to relax in his tiny cabin. Whenever there was even a hint that they were approaching enemy vessels, he remained awake in the tower on the bridge day and night, for if he had hesitated to dive for even a moment, he would have forfeited his chances of destroying the coveted prey. And so he learnt to get by without sleep and to rest for only a few brief seconds, when he would lie down in his wet clothes, constantly ready to react to the warning signal of the officer on watch.[10]

One such situation arose on 1 May, when the *U-20* approached the route taken by British liners on their way to the Firth of Forth on Scotland's east coast. The fog was so dense that Schwieger was unable to attack and so he gave the order to dive. The very next day he was again required to show great presence of mind when six British destroyers approached him over a wide front, and it was only at the very last moment that the *U-20* managed to reach a depth of 50 feet, where his submarine was safe. By the evening his batteries were so low that they had to be recharged on the surface. 'If destroyers had again been patrolling the area to the north of us,' Schwieger noted in his diary, 'our situation would have been critical as our battery was pretty nearly gone.'[11] By the time the *U-20* reached the North Atlantic shortly afterwards, the weather was fine. The crew's mood immediately improved.

On the promenade deck of the *Lusitania*, too, the mild spring air and pleasant Atlantic wind dispelled all sombre thoughts, most of the passengers having grown used to their new lives as part of a floating community. But third-class passengers such as twelve-year-old Elise Hook and her eleven-year-old brother, Frank, from Toronto soon discovered that there were social barriers on board. Their father, George Hook, had originally bought second-class tickets but when he discovered that his former housekeeper, Annie Marsh, together with her husband and son, was in third class, he decided that out of solidarity with them his family would join the Marshes in third class. A spirit of camaraderie quickly developed in the enormous third-class dining room, where passengers soon forged bonds with one another. Only a few small groups of Russian migrants kept themselves apart. They included the Antila family from the border area between Russia and Finland. After their failed attempt to enter the United States, they were being deported by the New York authorities together with their two small children. Their mood of desperation was lifted only a little by the twenty-six-year-old Iwan Michalkowicz from Chicago, who joined them at their table and informed them of his plans to enlist as a volunteer and fight the Germans in Europe.

On the evening of 3 May the stewards knocked on the doors of the first-class cabins, partly to check that the regulations for keeping the lights dimmed were being observed, but also to remind passengers of the gala dinner to which Captain Turner had invited them. Turner hoped that the dinner might help to distract his guests from some of the mishaps that had taken place over the course of the voyage so far, all of them due to the shortage of manpower that was in turn a result of the war. Among the reservists whom he had had to let go were some of his finest men, whereas many of their replacements had no training, and some of the stewards spoke only limited English. Turner had discussed these matters with his first officer, John Anderson, and at the same time had asked him to draw up a gala programme and compile a guest list, including a seating plan.

Although Anderson was more socially adept than his captain, even he had difficulty producing a meaningful mix of prominent figures from the worlds of finance, politics and the arts and devising a suitable seating plan. It was clear that Alfred Vanderbilt would sit at Turner's table. But who else? In general Turner struggled to engage in conversation with men and women from the world of culture and with intellectual heavyweights, especially with such exotic individuals as Frohman, the Hubbards and the American spiritualist Theodate Pope. It would no doubt have been more sensible to extend invitations to two shipping magnates, Paul Crompton of the Booth Steamship Company and Albert L. Hopkins of the Newport News Shipbuilding

Drydock Company, while female dinner guests might have included the American fashion designer Carrie Kennedy or Mary Crowther Ryerson, wife of the founder of the Canadian Red Cross. Others who might have been invited to the captain's table were Sir Hugh Lane, the Irish patron of the arts; Fred Stark Pearson, the American engineer and designer of a dam and irrigation project in Medina County, Texas; Marie Depage; and the president of the United States Chemical Company, Anne Shymer.

Anderson was immensely relieved to discover that the New York wine dealer and 'Champagne King' George Kessler was planning an on-board party that very same evening, making it possible to combine the invitations and relax the rules of protocol governing such events. The famous men and women from the world of the theatre were known to form their own cliques on such occasions, and so no particular seating plan was necessary for them. Their invitations needed only to ensure that Frohman, the Hubbards, Josephine Brandell and Rita Jolivet sat near the English actor and playwright Charles Klein, his American colleague Justus Forman and the English-born actress Amelia Herbert, who had married the American lawyer Henry D. Macdona in 1908. Anderson also thought it a good idea to organize separate seating plans for the diplomats, members of the clergy, scientists and journalists who were on board and who included the Reverend Basil Maturin, the Roman Catholic chaplain at the University of Oxford; Frederico G. Padilla, the Mexican consul general in Great Britain; the English polar explorer Joseph Foster

Stackhouse; the publisher and founder of the American literary magazine *The Chap-Book*, Herbert Stone; Frances Stephens, widow of the Canadian cabinet minister George Stephens; the bookseller Charles E. Lauriat and his colleague, the American historian and genealogist Lothrop Withington.

They all came with the intention of ensuring that the on-board party on 3 May 1915 was the social high point of their voyage – it was almost as if they suspected that it would be their last crossing. The guests made their slow and stately way across the red carpet leading from the foyer to the dining rooms, which extended over three floors. The main event was in the restaurant on D Deck, while individual receptions were held in the upper saloon beneath the high dome and between Corinthian marble columns on C Deck. The mood was one of calm, with no hint of an impending disaster. But late in the evening, while the on-board orchestra was playing dance tunes to mark the end of the official dinner, there was something of a scandal, when a sizeable group of younger passengers protested at the music of Johann Strauß. They wanted an American one-step – a ballroom dance marked by quick walking steps that was regarded as the precursor of the foxtrot – instead of a Viennese waltz. A handful of older couples left the saloon in the wake of this 'disturbance' and retired to their staterooms, and yet this was clearly not a musical reflection of the generation gap among the passengers but rather a symbolic expression of the wartime conflict between Austro-German 'culture' and western 'civilization'.

While fashionably new American dances were being tried out in the *Lusitania*'s ballroom, the *U-20* had reached a point to the west of the Hebrides and was beginning her long journey along the Scottish coast towards Ireland. The closer the submarine came to her planned hunting ground, the more often Schwieger had to ask his crew to stop singing their popular chorus, 'We're sailing off to Eng-e-land'. Extreme concentration was now of the essence. Schwieger's gramophone, too, no longer played the lively strains of the Radetzky March, which gave way to the tragic solemnity of Wagner's operatic choruses. When the submarine was on the surface, nothing could be allowed to distract the crew member on watch in the conning tower. A large Danish freighter had already escaped thanks to a moment of inattention, while a further attack failed when the torpedo became stuck in the launch tube. An attack on the neutral Swedish steamship *Hibernia* on 4 May likewise ended in failure.

But on 5 May it was finally possible to report a success, when the *U-20*'s gun crew sank a small British schooner, the *Earl of Lathom*, off the southern coast of Ireland. Her captain and four-man crew were able to escape by lifeboat. A similar scene unfolded on the morning of 6 May, when the *U-20* sank the 5,000-ton freighter *Candidate*. Again her crew managed to escape. Conversely, dense fog helped the 15,000-ton steamer, the *Arabic* of the White Star Line, make good her escape only a few hours later, but her stay of execution was to prove relatively brief, for she was sunk by another German U-boat only three months later –

in almost the same spot as the *Lusitania*. On the evening of 6 May, the *U-20* found another victim and without any preliminary warning torpedoed the British freighter the *Centurion* off Waterford. The vessel sank so slowly, however, that captain and crew were able to escape into lifeboats.

The activities of the *U-20* in the area the *Lusitania* was approaching were naturally registered by the local naval bases. On the evening of 6 May, for example, Captain Turner received a message from Queenstown, warning him of the presence of U-boats in the area, a warning that evidently came with instructions to reduce his speed. The British secret services were aware of Schwieger's official orders and of his activities in the Irish Sea and hoped that if the *Lusitania* reduced her speed she might avoid a dangerous encounter with a German submarine to the south of Ireland. Last-minute changes of direction by vessels approaching Queenstown were not out of the question. It has proved impossible to say for certain if Turner deliberately ignored routine instructions to plot a zig-zag course. Since October 1914 the British Admiralty's secret news agency ('Room 40') had been in possession of the codebooks relating to German naval and diplomatic communications, but there were repeated breakdowns in evaluating the material and a lack of coordination between the different departments. For safety's sake the external lighting on the *Lusitania* was turned off at night and the lifeboats were swung out from the sides of the ship, ready to be lowered as soon as the liner reached dangerous waters.

What neither the British naval base nor Captain Turner could know was that Schwieger had abandoned his official plan to lie in wait off Liverpool, or perhaps he had never intended to carry it out. The *U-20* was still lurking off the south coast of Ireland. His logbook entry for the evening of 6 May reads:

> The night is not entirely clear, making it impossible to keep watch for departing transport ships above water off Liverpool since accompanying destroyers cannot be identified in time, and it is to be assumed that some accompanied transport ships will leave Liverpool during the night. On our way to St George's Channel our consumption of fuel has already been so great that it would be impossible to return from Liverpool via the south of Ireland. I plan to return when we have used up two-thirds of our fuel. [...] We have only three torpedoes left, two of which I intend, if possible, to save for use on our journey home. It is decided, therefore, to remain to the south of the entrance to the Bristol Channel and attack steamers until down to two-fifths fuel.[12]

The steamship that Schwieger had his eye on – the *Lusitania* – was currently only around 100 nautical miles away and approaching quickly. Captain Turner had adopted special safety measures during the night of 6/7 May. The lookouts were changed every two hours and Turner addressed the passengers on the evening of the 6th in an attempt to reassure them, but many passengers spent a restless night. Early on the morning of the 7th the *Lusitania* passed the Fastnet Rock off Ireland's southern coast, but the outcrop was shrouded in dense fog and as a result it was invisible. By now visibility was reduced to 100 feet. Turner sounded the fog horn, chiefly to alert the cruiser *Juno*, which he assumed was in the vicinity because she had originally been ordered to escort the *Lusitania* to her destination; but the *Juno* had in fact been instructed to return to Queenstown. Late that morning the crew of the *U-20* heard the cruiser passing overhead. Twenty minutes later silence returned and Schwieger ordered his periscope to be raised. The fog had lifted, the sun was shining and the *Juno* had disappeared. For the *Lusitania* too, now twenty miles away, the fog had lifted to reveal a view of the Irish coast. Most of the passengers were in the dining rooms having lunch, only a few of them lingering on deck, unable to tear themselves away from the sight of land. They were standing by the rail of the promenade deck and watching through telescopes as the outlines of the Old Head of Kinsale grew increasingly clear. They would soon reach their destination. Captain Turner, too, felt relieved at the sight of the distinctive headland and its lighthouse. He was now only eighteen miles off the coast and barely twenty-five miles from Queenstown, where the *Juno* had docked without incident.

It was 1.20 pm when Schwieger sighted the *Lusitania* through his periscope. Some twelve miles ahead of him he noticed a trail of smoke and then a huge ocean-going liner 'over 25,000 tons', he noted in his logbook, 'with four funnels and two masts'.[13] For Schwieger and his pilot Rudolf Lanz it must have been clear at once that the liner was the *Lusitania*. She was currently sailing parallel to the coast at a speed that Schwieger reckoned was twenty knots, offering little chance that he would be able to come within firing range. But then something unexpected happened and the *Lusitania* suddenly turned thirty degrees to starboard. Clearly she was making directly for Queenstown, bringing her into the best possible position for a torpedo attack. Schwieger immediately gave orders for the *U-20* to dive and as stealthily as he could he headed for his target with the greatest possible speed. In order to achieve the best position to attack the *Lusitania*, his helmsman needed to calculate the correct depth for the U-boat. While the torpedo was being armed and prepared for launch, a tense silence descended on the submarine. When she was within 2,300 feet of the liner, Schwieger gave the order to fire. The submarine shuddered slightly as the torpedo left its launch tube with a hiss. Two propellers kept it from rolling and veering, while driving it forwards at a speed of twenty-two knots.

On board the *Lusitania*, the starboard lookout, Leslie ('Gertie') Morton, was the first to spot the danger: some 2,600 feet away he saw what he later described as 'a turmoil, and what looked like a bubble on a large scale in the water'. A few seconds later he saw 'two white streaks running along the top of the water like an invisible hand with a piece of chalk on a blackboard. They were heading straight across to intercept the course of [the] *Lusitania*.'[14] Morton grabbed his megaphone and called to the bridge, where his warning was met with incomprehension by the officers on duty, Percy Hefford and Albert Bestic. By the time they had passed on the message to Captain Turner, it was already too late. The torpedo struck the *Lusitania* below the waterline just in front of the bridge at the point at which the transverse and longitudinal bulkheads met. Behind them were the orlop deck and the reserve coal bunker. Turner likened the noise of the impact to the banging of a door on a windy day.

Shortly afterwards there was a second, far more violent explosion that produced fire and clouds of smoke. Wreckage and splinters of wood rained down on the startled and terrified passengers who were still on deck. The *U-20* drew closer to the sinking ship and circled it, while Schwieger impassively watched its death throes, which lasted eighteen minutes. Before retracting the periscope and heading for the open seas, he allowed a number of his crew members to observe the disaster. His war diary contains the following entry:

> There follows an extraordinary explosion with a very large cloud of smoke (far higher than the front smokestack). There must have been a second explosion after the torpedo hit home (boiler or coal or powder?). The bridge, together with those parts of the ship situated above the point of impact, are torn apart, fire breaks out and thick smoke envelops the high bridge. The ship stops abruptly and immediately starts to list noticeably to starboard, while the bows move lower in the water. It

looks as if she will capsize in a short space of time. There is great confusion on the ship: the boats are swung free and in some cases let down into the water. There must have been a great deal of panic; several boats, fully laden, are hurriedly lowered, bow or stern first, and at once fill with water.[15]

This matter-of-fact account gives no hint of the heart-rending scenes that unfolded on the deck of the *Lusitania* and in the waters around her. She began to list to starboard so quickly that those passengers who had been hit by flying debris were unable to get to safety, while the lifeboats could not be properly lowered into the water. By the same token, Captain Turner's desperate attempt to steer the stricken vessel towards the coast was bound to fail, for the *Lusitania* had lost control of her steering. The electricity supply had been cut immediately after the explosions, plunging the interior of the ship into darkness. Passengers streamed out on to the decks in panic, the lifts not infrequently becoming death traps. Many refused to return to their cabins for their life jackets. James ('Jay') Ham Brooks, a car salesman from Bridgeport, Connecticut, was close to the Marconi room, directly behind the bridge, when the torpedo struck. He himself was able to escape, but he later left a vivid description of the chaotic attempts to launch the lifeboats:

There was a dull explosion and a quantity of debris and water was flung into the air beside the bridge. The water-spout knocked me down by the Marconi office. This explosion was followed soon after by a second rumbling explosion entirely different from the first. [. . .]

The efforts made to lower the boats had not apparently met with much success. Those on the port side had swung inward and could not be used, while the collapsible boats, lashed between them, could not be reached.

Women were standing quite calmly, waiting for an opportunity to enter the boats when they should be released by the men from the davits. The davits, by this time, were touching the water, the ship having sunk so low. The bridge deck was only four feet or so from the surface of the sea.

Losing no time, the men passed the women rapidly into the boats, places having been found for all the people about the midship section. I stepped into one of the lifeboats and attempted to assist in getting it free. I saw that the list was so great that the davits pinched the gear, rendering it impossible for us to get away before the ship went down. So I dived into the water.

I swam as hard as I could, and noticed with feelings of apprehension the menacing bulk of the huge funnels as they loomed over my head. I expected them momentarily to fall and crush me, but at last I judged myself to be clear.

I turned around to watch the great ship heel over. The monster took a sudden plunge, and I saw a crowd still on her decks and boats filled with helpless women and children glued to her side. I sickened with horror at the sight.

> There was a thunderous roar, as of the collapse of a great building on fire: then she disappeared, dragging with her hundreds of fellow-creatures into the vortex. Many never rose to the surface, but the sea rapidly grew black with the figures of struggling men and women and children.[16]

There were also misunderstandings and well-meaning acts that had terrible consequences. The New York stockbroker Isaac Lehmann reports an incident that left him traumatized for many years afterwards. There was a large crowd of desperate passengers on the portside deck, where lifeboat no. 18, although full, was still hanging from its davit. A sailor had been instructed to knock out the restraining pin with an axe once the boat was level with the sea. But Lehmann, as he later regretfully recalled, felt that this was taking too long and so he forced the sailor at gunpoint to lower the boat forthwith. The sailor dislodged the pin, but just at that moment the whole ship lurched violently, causing the lifeboat to slide abruptly down the steep deck, crushing at least thirty people against the wall of the smoking room. Lehmann, too, sustained serious injuries to his leg.

It is clear from various reports and interviews with survivors that Alfred Vanderbilt and his valet Ronald Denyer were responsible for many acts of selfless heroism that saved the lives of others while resulting in their own deaths. Not only Vanderbilt but also the impresario Charles Frohman and Margaret Mackworth, an early champion of women's rights, are said to have turned down a seat in a lifeboat in favour of others. Shortly before the *Lusitania* went down, Vanderbilt removed his lifejacket and gave it to a desperate young woman. Charles Frohman revealed a comparable degree of calm or fatalism during the liner's final minutes. When the torpedo struck, he was sitting at a table in the Veranda Café with the actress Rita Jolivet, the singer and promoter George Vernon and the British naval officer Alick John Scott. When they realized the enormity of the disaster, they all went to stand by the rail of the promenade deck, where they planned to wait until the ship went down. Frohman declined to put on a lifejacket but lit a cigar and tried to calm the agitated Rita Jolivet, who later recalled that he was like a theatre director talking through a part with her. Then an enormous wave swept over the deck like an avalanche, tearing the four friends apart. Only Rita Jolivet survived.

Barely documented at all are the fates of third-class passengers and those crew members who stood little chance of surviving in the bowels of the ship. Among the few engineers and stokers who were able to escape were Eugene McDermott and Tom Madden. They told the Mersey Inquiry about their dramatic escape from the boiler rooms. The shock wave caused by the explosion almost deafened them, but they were both instinctively aware of the danger of being cooked alive by the escaping steam. Madden had been in Boiler Room 1 and reported that the wall between the front and middle coal bunkers on the starboard side burst like paper and seawater flooded in. Through choking dust and blinding steam he groped his way towards a door midships, but it refused to open. The rising waters swept him along like flotsam and jetsam. He clung to a crate of coal that was floating past and in that way was carried through the pitch-black boiler room to the starboard side of the ship, where he was able to reach the lowest rungs of the escape ladder and with his last remaining strength climb out on to the deck. McDermott was in Boiler Room 2 beneath the second smokestack. Here too the water broke in with tremendous force, snatching up a number of firemen and hurling them against the boilers or bulkheads. He saw how two of his comrades, William Mallin and Leslie Plummer, sustained fatal injuries in the impact. He himself was carried along by the dark water, almost 10 feet deep, until he reached the lower grille of an air vent, at the upper end of which he could see daylight. He managed to reach the ladder in the shaft and climb up to the deck beside the smokestack. He was the only survivor from Boiler Room 2.

One of the ship's officers, Albert Bestic, was still busy lowering the last lifeboat on the starboard side of the vessel when a huge wave, carrying debris and bodies on its crest, threatened to overwhelm him, too. Without thinking, he leapt overboard and swam for his life. A whirlpool seized him and dragged him down, the water appearing to change from green to black before his eyes. His ears seemed as if they would burst and he struck out desperately with his arms and legs until the water became clearer again. When he reached the surface, he was able to observe the *Lusitania*'s final moments. She sank slowly, bow first, exposing her propellers and rudder. Hundreds of men, women and children were still clinging to the afterdeck that towered up above him, while others plunged down and disappeared into the sea. He then heard a boiler explode, tearing down one of the funnels and releasing more clouds of black smoke.

The *Lusitania* was almost completely submerged when she made 'a peculiar lurching movement' and emitted a 'terrible moan'.[17] Bestic then saw the ship tremble one last time and glide vertically beneath the surface until she struck the seabed around 300 feet below the surface, the thunderous roar suggesting that her bowels had been ripped from her body. None of those passengers and crew who had been sucked down with her was seen again.

For a time the sea boiled with churning white water, before the surface grew calm once again, covering the grave of the *Lusitania* as if with a shroud. Of the liner's forty-eight lifeboats, only six had survived. Filled to overflowing with survivors, they floated on the almost calm waters. Bestic swam on his back and heard the cries of helpless men and women and the terrible whimpering of infants in their rocking baskets, to which lifejackets had been hastily tied. By the time he finally reached an empty upturned boat, the cries and whimpering had all but ceased and he had the impression of being completely alone. His memory of this dreadful scene continued to haunt him for the rest of his life.

Another passenger, the English architect and designer Oliver Bernard, who had been working in Boston prior to his return home, reported similarly traumatic scenes. In his youth he had spent two years at sea as a cabin boy on a Norwegian barque and had some experience of the use of lifeboats, experience that was to prove extremely useful during the *Lusitania* disaster. He was among the fortunate survivors who found refuge in one of the few undamaged lifeboats that was able to break free from the dangerous suction of the sinking ship. And yet he found it difficult to speak about what he had seen:

> It was one long scene of agony. There was floating debris on all sides, and men, women, and children clinging for dear life to deck chairs and rafts which littered the water. There were such desperate struggles as I shall never forget. Many were entangled between chairs, rafts, and upturned boats. One by one they seemed to fall off and give themselves up to death. One poor wretch was struck by the oar which I was sharing with a steward. We struck him full in the head but he seized and clung to the oar like grim death until we were able to drag him into the boat. Next we saw a woman floating quite near us. Her face was just visible above the water, and her mouth was covered with froth.[18]

Bernard and the other occupants of the boat were unable to help the woman, who died only a few minutes later. A young nurse who was likewise able to escape in a lifeboat reported having to watch helplessly as a screaming mother gave birth to her child in the water.

Captain Turner remained on his sinking ship until the very last moment, not jumping into the water until it was already washing over the bridge. What happened next has never been properly established as Turner himself barely spoke about it. According to one report, he clung first to an oar, then to a chair, while 'constantly fighting off attacks by sea-gulls' that 'swooped down on the dazed and benumbed people floating helpless on the surface and pecked their eyes out'. Finally, weakened by the cold and exposure, he 'flung up a gold-braided arm' to attract attention.[19] A crew member who was swimming nearby helped to hold his captain's head above water until a rescue vessel picked them up. His first officer John Anderson was not so fortunate: he went down with the ship, and his body was never found.

At 3.15 pm, a little over an hour after his attack on the *Lusitania*, Walther Schwieger's log reveals that he took one final dispassionate look at the events that he had caused: 'Astern in the distance, a number of lifeboats active; nothing more seen of the *Lusitania*.'[20] Within minutes he had turned his attention to a new victim, for he had seen a Cunard Line freight steamer close at hand and tried to sink it by firing a torpedo at its stern, but the torpedo missed its target, and the freighter continued its journey unawares. Evidently her captain had heard nothing about the danger or about the *Lusitania* disaster.

The Queenstown Graves

Even before the SOS had been received in Queenstown ('Come at once. Big List. 10 miles south Old Head Kinsale'),[21] fishermen and farmers had already been alerted to the tragedy off their coast by the dull explosions and rising cloud of black smoke. The crew of the little fishing cutter from the Isle of Man, the *Wanderer*, witnessed the drama. They had cast their nets only a few miles away and noticed that a huge liner that had sailed past them only shortly before was suddenly in difficulty after suffering a series of explosions. Not until later did they discover that it was the *Lusitania*. The *Wanderer* immediately set sail for the sinking ship and reached the scene of the tragedy before the flotilla of rescue vessels from Queenstown, with the result that she was able to save two hundred of the passengers and crew. Since the tiny cutter was itself in danger of sinking beneath the weight of all the rescued survivors, it towed two lifeboats in its wake. Eighteen more survivors were taken on board the trawler *Dan O'Connell*, which also happened to be in the area. But hundreds of other survivors had to wait several hours to be rescued by the fleet of twenty or so tugs, trawlers and torpedo boats assembled by Admiral Sir Charles Coke in Queenstown. With the onset of darkness the search was temporarily suspended. By then almost eight hundred survivors had been picked up and more than two hundred bodies recovered. Many of the victims had broken bones and serious injuries, with the result that a number of them died after they had been rescued.

In total 1,197 men, women and children lost their lives in the *Lusitania* disaster. Of these, 788 were registered passengers, including 128 Americans. Of the 693 crew members, 402 were killed. Ninety-four of the 129 children on board perished in the tragedy, including 35 of the 39 infants. There were only 767 survivors: 476 passengers and 291 crew members.

Compared to the daily losses in the land battles of the First World War, the number of victims of the *Lusitania* disaster seems relatively small, but their symbolic significance was unique. Apart from the appalling number of dead children, contemporaries registered above all the deaths of the many prominent figures from the worlds of business, politics, science and culture, losses that resulted in a sense of uncomprehending dismay. A selection of the best-known names reads like a who's who of British and American high society of the time: the American engineer, economist and writer Lindon Bates II (*1883); the American building contractor and investor Albert Bilicke (*1861); the general manager of the Scottish whisky distiller John Dewar and Sons, Alexander Campbell (*1871); William B. Cloete (*1851), a British businessman whose mining interests included the New Sabinas Company in Mexico; the president of the Booth Steamship Company, Paul Crompton (*1878); the English scientist and vice-president of the Earp–Thomas Farmogerm Company, Robert E. Dearbergh (*1867); the Belgian diplomat and founder of the École Belge d'Infirmières Diplômées, Marie Depage (*1872); the American writer and playwright Justus Forman (*1875), whose plays included *The Hyphen*; the American theatre producer Charles Frohman (*1860), who had staged Barrie's *Peter Pan*; the British art dealer and founder of the London-based jeweller's that bore his name, Edgar E. Gorer (*1872); the British-born American actress Amelia Herbert (*1856); the American shipbuilder and president of the Newport News Shipbuilding Drydock Company, Albert L. Hopkins (*1871); the American women's rights activist and writer Alice Moore Hubbard (*1861); the American writer, satirist and founder of the Roycroft artists' collective, Elbert Hubbard (*1856); the American fashion designer Carrie Kennedy (*1862); the English actor and playwright Charles Klein (*1867), whose melodramas, hugely successful in the early years of the twentieth century, include *The Lion and the Mouse*; the Irish patron of the arts and founder of Dublin's Municipal Gallery of Modern Art, Sir Hugh Lane (*1875); the Reverend Dr Basil Maturin (*1847), the Roman Catholic chaplain at the University of Oxford who had briefly been the rector at St Clement's Church in Philadelphia and who was the second cousin of Oscar Wilde; the Mexican consul general in the United Kingdom, Frederico G. Padilla (*1880); Frederick Pearson (*1861), a consulting engineer whose work included a dam and irrigation project at Medina County, Texas; the American industrialist Charles Plamondon (*1858); Mary Crowther Ryerson (*1860), the wife of Major General George Ryerson, the founder of the Canadian Red Cross; the American chemist and president of the United States Chemical Company, Anne Shymer (*1879); the British polar explorer and adventurer Joseph Foster Stackhouse (*1873); Frances Stephens (*1851), the widow of the Canadian cabinet minister George Stephens; the American editor and publisher Herbert Stone (*1872), who owned the publishing house of H. S. Stone & Company and whose magazines included *The Chap-Book* and *The House Beautiful*; the American multimillionaire and horse breeder Alfred Gwynne Vanderbilt (*1877); and Lothrop Withington (*1856), the American historian, genealogist and writer.

Queenstown assumed the air of a charnel house. The recovered bodies were placed in three makeshift morgues in the town, including the local town hall. The sight of the dead children laid out on wooden pallets like dolls was almost unbearable. Oliver Bernard later recalled that 'a number of babies, I should say about thirty, were laid out stark and stiff on the floor of a temporary morgue. I never saw anything quite so ghastly and harrowing, and it filled me with an insensate desire for vengeance. I hope those tiny mites will be fully avenged.'[22]

Other witnesses reported that most of the children at least looked peaceful, as if they had not suffered when they died. With every returning ship the morgues continued to fill.

The inhabitants of Queenstown and of the whole of the Irish coastal region were left profoundly shaken, anger, grief and compassion proving more powerful than their usual hostility to the English. Numerous young Irishmen spontaneously volunteered to serve in the British army. Communal institutions, together with local families and hotels, took in the traumatized survivors and donated clothes and food. Doctors, ambulance drivers and nurses tirelessly tended the injured. Three days after the disaster a two-mile procession through the streets of the town bade farewell to the victims. The bishop of Cobh, Robert Browne, had previously celebrated Mass in St Colman's Cathedral.

Carts and horses from the whole of County Cork were made available for the cortege, which drove out from the town to the old cemetery, where three mass graves had been dug. Heading the procession was a military band. The coffins were draped with the Union flag and accompanied by Protestant and Catholic clerics. All shops and offices were closed, and the ships in the harbour flew their flags at half mast. The road was lined with members of the local community, who listened reverently to the strains of Chopin's Funeral March. At the sight of the coffins the mourners remembered with a shudder that there were almost 1,000 bodies still unaccounted for in the Atlantic.

Two hundred coffins were blessed and buried in the Queenstown Cemetery, after which a guard of honour fired a salute and the mourners sang *Abide With Me*. As for the American dead and the many prominent victims of the disaster, arrangements had already been made for their bodies to be repatriated. The authorities and the local undertakers reportedly had great difficulty finding experts who could embalm all the bodies.

Gospel in New York

In New York it was nine o'clock in the morning when the *Lusitania* went down. The news spread quickly, as the American composer Charles Ives reported:

> I remember, going downtown to business, the people on the streets and on the elevated train had something in their faces that was not the usual something. Everybody who came into the office, whether they spoke about the disaster or not, showed a realization of seriously

experiencing something. (That it meant war is what the faces said, if the tongues didn't.) Leaving the office and going uptown about six o'clock, I took the Third Avenue 'L' at Hanover Square Station. As I came on the platform, there was quite a crowd waiting for the trains, which had been blocked lower down, and while waiting there, a hand-organ or hurdy-gurdy was playing in the street below. Some workmen sitting on the side of the tracks began to whistle the tune, and others began to sing or hum the refrain. A workman with a shovel over his shoulder came on the platform and joined in the chorus, and the next man, a Wall Street banker with white spats and a cane, joined in it, and finally it seemed to me that everybody was singing this tune, and they didn't seem to be singing in fun, but as a natural outlet for what their feelings had been going through all day long. There was a feeling of dignity all through this. The hand-organ man seemed to sense this and wheeled the organ nearer the platform and kept it up fortissimo (and the chorus sounded out as though every man in New York must be joining in). Then the first train came and everybody crowded in, and the song gradually died out, but the effect on the crowd still showed. Almost nobody talked – the people acted as though they might be coming out of a church service. In going uptown, occasionally little groups would start singing or humming the tune.

Now what was the tune? It wasn't a Broadway hit, it wasn't a musical comedy air, it wasn't a waltz tune or a dance tune or an opera tune or a classical tune, or a tune

> that all of them probably knew. It was (only) the refrain of an old Gospel Hymn that had stirred many people of past generations. It was nothing but – 'In the Sweet Bye and Bye'.[23]

As both man and artist, Ives was for a long time exercised by the fact that it was this Gospel tune that best captured the mood of New Yorkers on that day in May 1915, and 'In the Sweet Bye and Bye' is quoted in this context in a number of his later works. In 1919, for example, he headed the third movement of his Second Orchestra Set 'From Hanover Square North, at the end of a Tragic Day, the Voice of the People Again Arose'. The title was intended to indicate that when he heard New Yorkers raise their voices in chorus, it was the democratic aspect of the tragedy that had moved him. For Ives, democracy was not unanimity but a multiplicity of voices polyphonically intertwined.

Another, equally moving reaction to the catastrophe was Winsor McCay's animated film *The Sinking of the Lusitania*, which he completed in 1918 and which is still available on YouTube. McCay was born to Canadian parents in Michigan in 1869 and continues to be regarded as one of America's leading caricaturists, cartoonists and producers of animated films. Prior to the outbreak of the First World War characters such as those found in *Little Nemo* and *Gertie the Dinosaur* may have reflected the hectic pace of modern life and the fears of contemporary Americans, but they tended to be surreal and to have little to do with day-to-day politics. The *Lusitania* disaster changed McCay's life and work overnight. Overwhelmed by the tragic events of May 1915, he asked for leave of absence as William Randolph Hearst's chief cartoonist and used his own private means to make an animated propaganda film that was intended to persuade the American people to enter the war against Germany.

Since McCay was a perfectionist and had no intention of abandoning that trait, the film took far longer than planned. Almost three years were necessary to complete the twelve-minute film using 25,000 drawings, hundreds of original photographs and as many intertitles filling 900 feet of film. The result was a sensation, but it came too late to be used for propaganda purposes, for by the time that the film reached the country's theatres and cinemas, the war was drawing to a close and the American public no longer needed to be stirred into action, so certain were they of victory.

CHAPTER 4

Jubilation and Horror

In its daily bulletin of 8 May the German Admiralty announced that the *Lusitania* had been torpedoed and sunk off the Old Head of Kinsale but forbore to add any comment. On the other hand, the chief of the Admiralty Staff, Hugo von Pohl, refused to let slip the opportunity to congratulate Walther Schwieger and his crew in person and so he organized a lavish reception for them at Wilhelmshaven, the largest German naval base. The sailors on board the warships that were lying at anchor there were invited to add their voices to the celebrations, greeting the 'U-boat Vikings' with cheers when they sailed into port. And Crown Prince Wilhelm cabled enthusiastically to his father from his military headquarters in north-western France: 'Tremendous delight here at the torpedoing of the *Lusitania*. [. . .] The more ruthlessly the U-boat war is waged, the quicker the war will end.'[1]

The German press, too, was triumphant: the *Frankfurter Zeitung*, the *Neue Preußische Zeitung* and the *Kölnische Zeitung* all spoke with one voice when hailing a 'justified' attack on an 'armed' ship that had had munitions and Canadian soldiers on board. The sinking of the *Lusitania* was also of moral significance, the papers went on, and a necessary response to British attempts to starve the German people with their blockade. British pride and indifference, together with Cunard's greed, were solely to blame for the tragedy. The *Westfälische Tageszeitung* struck a particularly cynical note: 'Our U-boats have finally made a significant catch. [. . .] We Germans are heartily pleased at this successful blow and regard with a wry smile the general howls of anger and screams of indignation. [. . .] No sentimentality: just a fight to the finish with this nation of vulgar shopkeepers.'[2]

In stark contrast to the German chorus of jubilation were the bitterness and indignation felt in Britain and America. The English papers spoke of the 'moral depravity' of the Germans, who could no longer be numbered among the civilized nations of the world. Particularly graphic were the reports in the *Daily Chronicle*. Terrible pictures of the dead were reproduced as evidence of 'the Hun's most ghastly crime',[3] and many papers printed shocking conversations with the survivors. It was Kaiser Wilhelm himself who had famously compared his compatriots with Huns when in 1900 he had demanded that German soldiers suppress the Boxer Uprising in China with the same degree of brutality as that evinced by Attila a thousand years earlier. Fifteen years later American newspapers, too, drew on this image. The *New York Herald* described the sinking of the *Lusitania* as 'premeditated murder',[4] while the *New York Times* expressed the view that 'in the history of wars there is no single deed comparable in its inhumanity and its horror'.[5]

The *Minneapolis Journal* added its voice to the chorus of indignation: 'Germany intends to become the outlaw of nations. Perhaps we are yet to witness savagery carried to its ultimate perfection.'[6] The German ambassador to the United States, Count Johann Heinrich von Bernstorff, was forced to cancel a planned visit to a gala performance of *Die Fledermaus* at the Metropolitan Opera that was intended to raise funds for the German Red Cross since he was held prisoner in the Ritz-Carlton Hotel, furious New Yorkers and reporters besieging the building and demanding an explanation from the German diplomat.

In Liverpool, London and almost every other major British city outraged citizens indiscriminately looted shops that had German or even vaguely German-sounding names. Windows were smashed and the contents of the shops thrown out into the street. In Liverpool it was dockworkers who led the demonstrations, while in London stockbrokers in their top hats headed a march on Parliament to demand that all Germans living in the country be interned. Even South Africa was gripped by a wave of protests, during which furious demonstrators in Johannesburg, Cape Town and Durban set fire to the homes of German immigrants. Walter Hines Page, the American ambassador in London, cabled Woodrow Wilson in Washington: 'The United States must declare war or forfeit European respect.'[7]

Even the newspapers in neutral countries were appalled at the Germans' unrestricted submarine warfare. The Norwegian *Morgenbladet*, for example, wrote that 'The news of the sinking of the *Lusitania* puts all other events in the shade and arouses the whole world to a feeling of horror. The Germans have meant to terrify. They have terrified their friends, and terror breeds hate.'[8] And on 15 May 1915 the Danish *Illustreret Tidende* expressed the contradictory and impotent feeling of 'neutrality' by drawing a comparison between the fate of the *Lusitania* and the loss of the *Titanic*:

> Politically speaking, Denmark must remain strictly neutral. This is necessary for our survival, but we cannot shackle our feelings of humanity in the face of our own consciences – to do so would be both unworthy and dishonest. When an invincible natural force in the form of an iceberg shattered the bow of the *Titanic* and caused the deaths by drowning of a large number of innocent and unsuspecting people, the entire world felt horror and compassion for those unfortunate souls. Now the same thing has happened again: once more an ocean liner has sunk with men, women and children who are innocent victims of the war – on this occasion, however, the disaster was caused by a deliberate act of will by a warmongering nation that presumes to determine the rules of engagement. All human understanding and all human standards fail us, making it impossible for us to grasp the enormity of this disaster. The waves of the sea have closed over the unfortunate passengers and the water has destroyed all trace of them. But this event will be engraved on the hearts of all civilized nations for all time, and nothing, nothing will ever be able to expunge it.[9]

Thomas Mann 'did not shed a tear'

Thomas Mann had only contempt for such 'sentimentality'. As famous as they are infamous, his *Reflections of a Nonpolitical Man* were written under the immediate impression of the *Lusitania* disaster and the effects of the U-boat war. Mann sought to defend the frenzy of nationalist celebrations as compared to their enemies' 'moral pussyfooting': 'The German people, *as* a people, [. . .] have not whined about what the radically merciless enemies have done to them in turn, but in an emergency they have not doubted their right to revolutionary measures, either; they have approved of such measures, and more than approved.' They sanctioned not only 'the march into Belgium' but also

> the destruction of that impudent symbol of English mastery of the sea and of a still comfortable civilization, the sinking of the gigantic pleasure ship, the 'Lusitania', and they defied the world-resounding hullabaloo that humanitarian hypocrisy raised. And they have not only approved of unlimited submarine warfare, they have cried for it and were bitter with their leaders almost to the point of rebellion when they hesitated to allow it to go on.[10]

In much the same spirit the popular writer and war reporter Ludwig Ganghofer poured scorn on foreign indignation:

> Years ago, one Shrove Tuesday, I saw a masked ball in a madhouse. I was reminded of this unspeakable mixture

> of tragic horror and grotesque comedy when I read the foreign accounts of the torpedoing of the *Lusitania*, accounts that took the form of despatches from Italy, of sentimental effusions on the part of English ministers, of radio broadcasts from the Eiffel Tower and of a solemn but artificially inflated speech by the noble but pallid Gaby D'Annunzio, to say nothing of the reports on those instructive cultural documents in which we are bound to see Anglo-Saxon attempts to expose us as German barbarians.[11]

And yet even in Germany there was shame, indignation and grief. While Thomas Mann was praising the 'edifying excellence' of Ganghofer's various writings, which achieved a print-run of more than half a million copies in 1915 alone, the satirist Karl Kraus was attacking Bavaria's frontline poet by portraying him in *The Last Days of Mankind* as a naïvely servile 'yodelling' war propagandist. When the war broke out, Kraus had still been a conservative advocate of the Habsburg monarchy and an admirer of the heir apparent, Franz Ferdinand, but the *Lusitania* disaster led him to revise his views completely. He initially said nothing on the subject but then launched an attack on the German Kaiser, accusing him of delusions of grandeur, incompetence and sadism.

Kraus spent the summer of 1915 preparing a special issue of his periodical *Die Fackel*, 'The End of the World in Black Magic', and also began work on *The Last Days of Mankind*, a play about the First World War made up of more than two hundred brief scenes featuring innumerable real and fictitious characters and designed to expose the absurdity and inhumanity of war. The work has no clear narrative structure. More than one third of the text consists of quotations assembled at random in the manner of a montage and taken from newspapers, sentences handed down by the country's courts and military orders. According to Kraus himself, 'Even the most unlikely deeds that are reported here actually happened; I have merely portrayed what these people did. Even the most unlikely conversations that are reproduced here were spoken word for word; the most lurid fantasies are quotations.'[12] Many scenes were illustrated as 'apparitions' and included the moving description of the *Lusitania* victims:

> A sweet sound. Dead calm after the sinking of the *Lusitania*. On a piece of floating wood, two children's corpses.
>
> The *Lusitania* Children:
> 'We pitch and toss upon the brine,
> Who knows where now we dwell –
> And yet how bright this life doth shine
> And children's cares dispel –!'[13]

The instinctive reaction was to demand that 'Tirpitz be torpedoed too', but Kraus felt that this was 'misguided because experience has taught us that in such cases it is not military objects but decent people who are affected'. Rather, he hoped that 'the image of the two children's bodies from the *Lusitania*' would 'haunt the admiral for the rest of his life'.[14] Even after the office of censor had been abolished in Austria and Germany, Kraus felt that his play would never be stageworthy. It was, he believed, 'unperformable'. And its stage history has proved him right. Even ambitious and more recent adaptations such as Johann Kresnik's attempt to stage the play in the Valentin submarine bunker in Bremen in 1999 failed to paper over the cracks between documentary and satire.

Within months of the end of the First World War the German writer and satirist Kurt Tucholsky had recognized that the Germans were evidently capable of no more than histrionic sentimentality. In 1919, performing at his cabaret in Berlin, he had asked his sentimental audience whether they had 'wept when the *Lusitania* had been torpedoed? When people were murdered on the cold high seas? Swallowing water and drowning?' Most Germans had not wept but instead had celebrated the loss of the liner. Even at one of the principal watering holes of Berlin's artist community, the Café des Westens, the Social Democrat journalist Felix Stössinger had loudly acclaimed the sinking of the *Lusitania* as 'the greatest act of heroism in the whole of human history'.[15] The response, however, had been one of indignation. The writer Leonhard Frank, who in 1914 had won the Fontane Prize for his socio-critical debut novel *The Robber Band*, strode over to Stössinger and without saying a word struck him in the face. Threatened with arrest, he then fled to Switzerland, where he wrote a number of short stories about the war. Collected together, they were published in Switzerland under the title *Man is Good*. In Germany, conversely, they were banned and could be imported only illegally. Opponents of the war disseminated copies and organized an event in Berlin at which the actress Tilla Durieux read from them. For a time Frank was a member of the Executive Committee of the Workers' and Soldiers' Council in Munich and was wounded when the movement was brutally suppressed in May 1919. After 1933 he was forced to flee to Switzerland for a second time. He spent his years of exile in London, Paris, Los Angeles and New York, before returning to Germany in 1950. He received numerous literary awards on both sides of a divided Germany but remained stateless until his death in Munich in 1961. Paradoxically, his very statelessness reveals a number of points in common with his former antagonist Felix Stössinger, for Stössinger, too, was an active member of the Workers' and Soldiers' Councils and from 1918 to 1922 edited the party newspaper of the Berlin branch of the Independent Social Democrats. He, too, was driven into exile in Switzerland after 1933.

The striking contradiction between Stössinger's socio-political sympathies and his blinkered German nationalism may be attributed to his Jewish ancestry and to the identity crisis that this background produced in him. Like many German Jews, Stössinger viewed the First World War as a chance to replace the prejudices that traditionally hampered relations between Christians and Jews with a unifying patriotism. Like the Jewish philosopher Hermann Cohen he pinned his hopes in 1915 on 'the triumph of

German weaponry'. But even in the later 1920s he was still complaining about 'Anglo-Saxon imperialism' and describing it as the 'cultural ideology of world dominion', seeing the 'danger of anti-Semitism' not in Germany but exclusively in the Soviet Union.[16]

The literary scholar Hans Mayer detected a curious Judaeo-German contradiction between education and political awareness in his uncle Ludwig Mayer, who was not only able to quote Heine and the German classics by heart but was also familiar with the literature of the English-speaking world. Politically speaking, however, this 'German Jewish representative of Enlightenment ideas' was 'a credulous nationalist who believed everything that the wartime propagandists would have us believe and who faithfully passed on that understanding to others'. In May 1915 this resulted in a 'terrible scene' at the supper table, when 'Uncle announced with an air of jubilation that German U-boats had sunk the American liner the *Lusitania*'. Mayer's father had been 'more excited' than he had ever seen him before and 'had said something I was never to forget: "We shall die in achieving victory!"'[17]

Erich Mühsam: 'Horror raised to its highest pitch'

The Jewish writer and anarchist Erich Mühsam revealed an equally far-reaching and clear-sighted view of the danger posed by the 'cultural ideology' of the German Reich. Even the symbolic title *Cain* that he gave to his 'journal for humanity' in 1911 signals the topicality of the biblical story of jealousy, fratricide and exile. When the First World War broke out, Mühsam suspended publication of his journal under the threat of censorship and instead resumed work on his diary, which he had broken off in November 1912. The drama of wartime events initially drove Mühsam, too, to lose all sense of direction. Although he had recognized the danger of war at a very early date and realized that civilization was at risk of breaking down completely, he had certainly not reckoned on the ebullient euphoria that gripped even him. And so we find him writing in his diary on 3–4 August 1914:

> And I, the anarchist, the anti-militarist, the enemy of nationalistic slogans, the anti-patriot and the rabid critic of the current frenzy to rearm, I find myself somehow moved by the general sense of intoxication, fired by a furious passion that may not be directed at any particular 'enemies' but which fills me with the burning desire to save 'ourselves' from them. But who are they? And who are 'we'?[18]

A few months later, on 11 December, Mühsam criticized the prince of anarchists, Pyotr Kropotkin: 'He's in Russia, fighting on behalf of the government in the belief that freedom is about to dawn on the nations of the world. As Reitze [the Swiss anarchist Albert Reitze] has already informed me, he is to proclaim the annihilation of the German "barbarians". The delusions of old age or a lapse from what is right and idealistic?'[19]

Gradually, however, Mühsam was able to distance himself from this mood of 'frenzy' and to feel only embarrassment at his confused state of mind during the early months of the war. It was a painful process as he tried to gain an objective and realistic overview of the conflict. He was unable to serve on the front as the army had no wish to have such an infamous anarchist in its ranks. He was given a medical examination but was not conscripted. He read the newspapers and discussed the war with friends such as Gustav Landauer, Frank Wedekind and Heinrich Mann, in addition to which he corresponded with Karl Liebknecht on the foundation of an International Cultural Association Against the War. His diary now served a new purpose, helping its author to put into words his inner fears and his feeling of incomprehension. The result is one of the most invaluable chronicles about the reality of the First World War, dealing, as it does, not only with the hostilities themselves but also with the personal despair of all those who were affected by the conflict.

For Mühsam, too, it was the *Lusitania* disaster that shocked him into revising his attitude to the war. His diary contains more than twenty entries on the subject, all of them attesting to the way in which the terrible events of May 1915 influenced everyday perceptions and relations between individuals. The first entry is dated Monday 10 May 1915:

> If it is possible for horror to get any worse and for it to be raised to its highest pitch, then the torpedoing and

> sinking of the English ocean liner the *Lusitania* is arguably the very pinnacle of horror. The ship, with 1,978 persons on board, two thirds of whom were passengers, a good half of them women, children and babes in arms, has been destroyed by a German U-boat in the Irish Sea. Of course, it is being said that the ship was armed (a point that the British Admiralty disputes) and had vast amounts of wartime munitions on board, and of course the German ambassador in America warned passengers against crossing the war zone on board British ships, a warning that has elicited the contempt of anti-German newspapers. So it is possible that from the standpoint of the conventions of war this appalling murder cannot be challenged. And yet it disgusts me to have to look for right and wrong when every human feeling is bound to cry out in horror. What a sense of grief was felt throughout the world three years ago when the *Titanic* struck an iceberg. Today we are far from feeling grief. 'Sheer delight,' the *Münchner Zeitung* observed, because the ingenious spirit of German technology has been able to devise machines that far outdo any iceberg and because a spirit of German heroism has learnt to use these machines safely and effectively without any feeling of false shame. O shame before the stars in the firmament![20]

The very next day he returned to the subject:

> The story of the *Lusitania* seems to have dealt the coup de grâce to Germany's standing in the world. And of

> course, no one at home or abroad is blaming the war for turning decent men and women into murderers and criminals. No, it is the *salles boches*, the German barbarians, who are being blamed in America, the Netherlands, Switzerland and, more especially, in 'enemy' countries, whereas we ourselves are blaming perfidious Albion. Any agreement is impossible, because here at home people accept the formal conventions of war as inherently decent, while refusing to abide by them themselves and as far as the outside world is concerned judging the murder of babies independently from the Hague Convention. [. . .] Italy still seems undecided, also Romania. But we shall presumably have to get used to war as a permanent institution. And everyone is waging it in the name of true culture, supreme morality and a Christianity that its champions claim they alone have correctly understood.[21]

An entry of 12 May 1915 indicates that when he visited Frank Wedekind at the Josephinum Clinic in Munich, where Wedekind was recovering from surgery, the two men talked about the war. Wedekind, whom Mühsam numbered among his 'true friends', shared his views with the diarist:

> He too sees the greatest danger in the militarization of Europe as the result of a German victory and spoke very forcefully about the terrible punishments meted out by the irregular soldiers in Belgium and about the submarine war, especially the case of the *Lusitania*. A number

> of his comments have stuck in my mind, including this one: 'It wouldn't surprise me if the war were soon to be conducted with poison and chemicals alone.'[22]

On 14 May 1915 Mühsam reported on the 'new orgies of violence directed against Germany' that had broken out in England by way of a reaction to the sinking of the *Lusitania*:

> Shops are being attacked, the Germans are being terribly persecuted and new countermeasures are being devised in the form of retribution on German prisoners. In other words, they are trying to defeat barbarism with barbarism – only in this way can our ruthless politicians improve their position. And yet no one is being told that there are many people in Germany who are as appalled by the monstrous nature of the U-boat war as the rest of the world, but the state of military despotism in which we currently find ourselves is preventing us from speaking. Things look incredibly sad in the world.[23]

Mühsam's diary entry of 17 May 1915 refers to a protest note from the American government and to 'further measures' by the English:

> The German papers are evidently prevented from reproducing it, but I read about it in the *Neue Zürcher Zeitung*. It is very strongly worded and emphatically denies Germany the right to conduct the U-boat war in the forms that have been practised hitherto. At the same

time it demands compensation. It is claimed that under international law torpedoing merchant vessels without prior warning but simply because they are suspected of carrying contraband is expressly forbidden. The note very clearly refers to the violation of the obligations of humanity and justice. Of course, the German government will back Tirpitz, and they will continue to commit such heinous acts. But for my own part I cannot get over the fact that every piece of villainy by our military leaders invariably stems from an earlier one, so that any attempt to apportion blame and establish innocence is a complete waste of time. Such horrors are simply a consequence of war. [. . .] In response to the torpedoing of the *Lusitania* the English government has once again ordered the arrest of all Germans that it can lay its hands on, and in England and South Africa outraged crowds have set fire to and looted all the German properties they have been able to reach – and this in turn has meant that we too have been suitably outraged. Everyone is right, of course: they are all barbarians. Everyone has been attacked in the most dastardly way: every country by its own government.[24]

Mühsam's diary entries of 25 and 28 May 1915 deal with central problems in his private life, although these, too, were affected by the events surrounding the *Lusitania*. Among Mühsam's many complicated relationships with women were two that needed clarifying at this time: his long-term affair with the 'delightfully natural' thirty-one-year-old

Kreszentia Elfinger ('Zenzl') and his passing fancy for the 'badly brought up' artist Fifi Elbogen from Vienna:

> My private life is permanently marked by two things: first, my financial worries, with the almost insuperable difficulties involved in bringing some sense of order to my life and in forming a union with Zenzl – and, second, the case of Fifi. Both women were here yesterday, and the impossibility of maintaining my relationship with Fifi became terribly clear when compared to my relations with Zenzl, who is so completely natural, unaffected and unspoilt in comparison. [. . .] A conversation about the *Lusitania* affair opened my eyes. When I told Fifi of my horrified dismay at the murder of so many children and women, all she could say was that at a time when so many men were falling in battle, it was perhaps a good thing that this was offset by the deaths of women and children.[25]

This conversation took place on 25 May. Within three days Mühsam had sorted out his private life, visiting Fifi Elbogen and reporting afterwards that

> My separation from Fifi was painful and awkward. It's the first time in my life that my relationship with a woman has ended badly for me. [. . .] I felt the need to discuss the matter as honestly and as comprehensively as possible, which is why I dealt in detail with the points that divide us and that had emerged so clearly from my

> conversation about the *Lusitania* in the English Garden. On that occasion her calculating attitude to the disaster had left me terribly upset, and my irritability turned to extreme hostility.[26]

With Zenzl, conversely, Mühsam spent a number of 'very, very sweet hours', marrying her only a few months later. The entry in his diary for 15 September 1915 reads simply: 'Married.'[27] The daughter of a landlord and brewer from Upper Bavaria, Zenzl Elfinger not only shared Mühsam's feelings of sympathy for the victims of the *Lusitania* disaster, she became an emancipated political champion of the Munich Soviet Republic, and while her husband was in prison she fought tirelessly for the incarcerated revolutionaries in her attempts to obtain an amnesty. Her life, like that of Mühsam himself, was to end tragically: following Mühsam's murder in the Oranienburg concentration camp in 1934, she fled via Prague to Moscow, only to find herself exiled by Stalin to a series of Soviet gulags, where she spent almost twenty years for alleged 'counterrevolutionary Trotskyite activities'. She was finally released in 1954 and allowed to travel to the German Democratic Republic, where she died in 1962. With the end of the GDR, the urn containing her ashes was transferred to her husband's grave in the Waldfriedhof in Berlin's Dahlem district.

A shared sense of indignation at the insults doled out to the victims of the *Lusitania* disaster in May 1915 had led to the union of Erich Mühsam and Kreszentia Elfinger four months later. The subject was to occupy the diarist until

September 1916. He discussed the legality and morality of the submarine war with friends and adversaries. One such friend was Ludwig Thoma, who before the war had co-edited the journal *März* with Hermann Hesse. Thoma also contributed to the satirical weekly *Simplicissimus* and was widely regarded as a left-wing liberal critic of society, Church and State. But with the outbreak of war he revised his position and it was with evident enthusiasm that he volunteered to work as a medical orderly on the eastern front. In a diary entry dated 9 July 1915 Mühsam reports on a 'two-hour conversation' with Thoma in the Hofgarten in Munich:

> Thoma is a medical orderly and was here on leave from Galicia. It's interesting talking to him as he represents the official line in government patriotism. It's not every day that you hear the kind of belligerent enthusiasm that this *Simplicissimus* revolutionary is currently spouting. He positively beamed at the mention of the *Lusitania*. The first dead Russian that he saw left no impression on him. It was good that the man was gone – that was his only feeling. He is in raptures over the U-boat war. The war will end when all our enemies have been defeated etc. – I vigorously defended my own standpoint but have to admit that Thoma's phlegmatic stance was completely unaffected by it.[28]

Following the *Lusitania* disaster Mühsam appears to have broken off contact with former colleagues such as Thomas

Mann who were enthusiastic advocates of Germany's U-boat war. In early February 1915 he had attended a public reading of Mann's *Thoughts in Time of War* in Munich's Steinicke Hall and gained the impression that Mann was 'heaping all virtues on Germany and – in the most unchivalrous way – all vices on all foreigners'. In his introduction Mann had 'confessed to believing in the gospel of the purest aesthetics' and done so 'in the most emphatic form imaginable'. In the case of Heinrich Mann, conversely, form was a 'precondition', not an end in itself, which was why he was 'much more important and more worthwhile than his brother'.[29]

Mühsam also expressed his enthusiasm at a lecture on Émile Zola that Heinrich Mann delivered on 25 June 1915 – Mann presumably read from the manuscript of the article that appeared the following November in René Schickele's *Die weißen Blätter*:

> Affinity and admiration were in evidence here, hence the fact that the fire radiated by the subject under discussion was communicated to the listener. By way of an introduction Mann made a few splendid remarks about the duty of intellectuals to reforge the spiritual bonds between nations. A few sensible remarks touched on the idea of an inner connection between intellectuals and the people, a connection that Mann regards as an expression of democracy. What he said moved me and uplifted me. It was beautiful, courageous and powerful.[30]

In the face of further 'U-boat crimes' in the eastern Mediterranean similar to the attack on the *Lusitania*, Mühsam came to view Heinrich Mann's idea of 'reforging the spiritual bonds between nations' as an active invitation to outlaw the German and Austrian governments. The most recent 'heroic outrage' had taken place on 30 December 1915, when a passenger liner, the *Persia*, was torpedoed and sunk off the coast of Crete with the loss of 343 passengers and crew, including numerous women and children. Among high-profile victims were the American senator and consul designate of Aden, Robert N. McNeely; the aspiring English actress Isabella Fladgate; the adviser to the Maharaja Jagatjit Singh, Inder Singh; the matron in charge of the Dufferin Hospital in Lahore, Elizabeth E. Smith; and Eleanor Thornton, the mistress of the Conservative politician and publisher Lord Beaulieu. (Beaulieu himself survived.) The ship was sunk by German U-boat *U-38* under the command of the notorious Max Valentiner. The passengers were having lunch when the torpedo struck the engine room without warning, causing a huge explosion. The ship listed to port and sank so quickly that – as with the *Lusitania* – most of the passengers had no time to reach the lifeboats.

A dismayed Mühsam noted in his diary on 4 January 1916 that the *Persia* 'had not been transporting weapons or munitions', that she was 'not armed', that she 'offered no resistance' and that 'no warning' had been given prior to the attack. 'Hundreds of people, including a large number of women and children', had been 'treacherously murdered for the sake of a few bags of mail'. And all of this had happened after the 'central governments' responsible for this and other actions had 'already been exposed by the atrocities associated with the *Lusitania*, the *Arabic* and the *Ancona*'. No one should ever 'associate with the governments of these countries, whether in the guise of treaties or any other agreements'. Heinrich Mann was right:

> In the case of all these nations, the idea of the state is now grotesquely inflated, destroying every humane and decent emotion and uncritically accepting whatever may serve to reinforce this idea. The German Reich as a political organization, the Hohenzollern dynasty, military force, everything is more important to our country than right and character. For these chimerical ideas it is ready to sanction every crime and even to commit such crimes itself.[31]

On 29 March 1916 Mühsam returned to the same point in a further diary entry: 'Every day new atrocities are being reported. French, English, Dutch and Norwegian passenger liners are simply sunk without warning. The *Lusitania* practice has triumphed.'[32]

Karl Liebknecht's Leaflet

The '*Lusitania* practice' exercised the German Reichstag more than any other wartime atrocity, for all that information about the sinking was controlled by military censorship. On 28 May 1915, for example, a parliamentary debate on Italy's entry into the war was launched in the Reichstag, while a pamphlet was being distributed outside the building. Its title, 'The Main Enemy is at Home!', was soon to become well known.

> You have been given no influence over Germany's and Austria's negotiations with Italy, negotiations on which Italy's intervention depends. You have been treated like sheep in this vital question, while the war party, secret diplomacy and a handful of people in Berlin and Vienna have rolled the dice to decide the fate of Germany.
>
> The torpedoing of the *Lusitania* has not only consolidated the power of the English, French and Russian war parties, it has invited a grave conflict with the United States and set all neutral countries against Germany, inspiring in them a sense of passionate outrage. But it has also facilitated the baleful work of the Italian war party at a particularly critical moment – on this point, too, the German people have been required to remain silent: the iron fist of the state of siege has been held tight around their throats.[33]

The anonymous author was the Social Democrat member of the Reichstag, Karl Liebknecht. His radical opposition to the current political truce led not only to his isolation in parliament but also to his exclusion from the Social Democratic faction. He described the mood in his party as 'so hostile to England' as to be indistinguishable from that of the bourgeois right. Most of his parliamentary colleagues had insisted that England was 'largely to blame for the sinking of the *Lusitania*' and had even asked 'if England had deliberately provoked this sinking in order to precipitate a new witch-hunt against Germany'.[34]

The authorities had already tried to silence Liebknecht in March 1915 by conscripting him and sending him to the eastern front as a non-combatant equipment service soldier, even though he was a member of both the Reichstag and the Prussian House of Representatives. Fortunately, he survived the Russian bullets, while his notoriety ensured that he had enough free time to read the newspapers, write letters and even gather political experience. 'The mood among non-combatant soldiers is highly charged and there is even a feeling of outrage,' Liebknecht wrote to his wife Sophie. They were 'all sick of the whole disgusting mess', the only exception being the army leaders. Within days of his arrival at the front 'all manner of officers, including two princes' had 'turned up to discuss the situation while the cannons thundered in the background'. Both parties had declined to mince their words:

> I spoke bluntly and in return they admitted to the German-Austrian attack, describing the murder of the crown prince at Sarajevo as a true blessing and uninhibitedly advocating the goal of conquest, one of them even confessing that for years he had been working towards the goal of war and that the war would last another year or so.[35]

Although Liebknecht had to be given leave of absence to attend sessions of the Reichstag and of the Prussian House of Representatives, his main problem was the official ban on all political activity outside parliament, including in his free time and while he was on leave. In spite of this he played a significant role in founding the group that later became known as the Spartacus League. In the spring of 1916 he tried to speak in a series of parliamentary debates on Tirpitz's resignation and on its consequences for unrestricted submarine warfare, but on each occasion he was prevented from doing so and was even physically assaulted, with the result that he was able to express his views only in writing. In a 'Letter from the Spartacus Group' dated 15 April 1916, we read:

> International law lies in the gutter, smashed to smithereens. The whole idea of regulating the madness associated with war has proved to be a foolish illusion. To hail its regulations as magic formulas capable of averting the dangers of submarine warfare is the preserve of those politicians who have learnt nothing from the most serious sermon of the world war and who at best want to replace the politics of destroyed illusions with the politics of new illusions. The claim that international law must also apply to the U-boat war implies that, with the exception of the U-boat war, the rules of international law are actually in force today.[36]

In spite of the obstacles that were placed in their path, Liebknecht and the other members of his group succeeded in organizing a protest demonstration on the Potsdamer Platz in Berlin on 1 May 1916, where they were joined by several thousand young workers and soldiers. Liebknecht was singled out by the police and arrested when he shouted 'Down with the war! Down with the government! Long live peace!' Heinrich Mann, too, was in Berlin at this time and reported afterwards that

> it is said that 20,000 protestors took part in the May demonstration on the Potsdamer Platz and that there was bloodshed when the police – not the boys of the Defence Force [a pre-military youth organization] – fired into the crowd. A large number of butchers' shops in the Wilhelmsdorfer Straße in Charlottenburg were torn down: in short, the mood certainly gives cause for hope.[37]

Although Mann's figures were exaggerated, the military authorities were undoubtedly surprised at the fact that an anti-war demonstration had taken place at all and that it was even registered abroad. On 12 May 1916, for example, the Dutch daily *Nieuws van den Dag* published a detailed article on the 'violent suppression of the German peace movement'. Similar reports were carried by the *Daily Telegraph*, *L'Humanité* and the *Berner Tagwacht*, while the Italian magazine *La Domenica Illustrata* even published a series of photographs in its edition of 14 May, its aim being to prove that the protest had resulted in '25 deaths and 200 injuries'. In the event, the fact that reports of the demonstration and copies of the protestors' leaflet had found their way abroad had a negative impact on the court's verdict on Liebknecht, who was accused of 'offering resistance' and of committing 'treason'. He was stripped of his parliamentary privileges and initially sentenced to two and a half years in prison, a sentence revised on appeal to four years and one month. In his appeal Liebknecht asked: 'Why does the indictment say nothing about the fact that shortly after I was arrested a few patriots – evidently disciples of the secret society associated with Herr von Jagow [the chief of police in Berlin] – beat me about the head with their walking sticks, while one of their number commented contentedly: "It was high time that we got him."'[38]

Liebknecht was released as part of a general amnesty in October 1918, but in the wake of the Spartacists' January Uprising ten weeks later, he and his comrade in arms, Rosa Luxemburg, were dragged away by soldiers belonging to the Guard Cavalry Rifle Division, who tortured and brutally murdered them. It is now clear that they were executed with the approval of the military representative of the new Social Democratic government, Gustav Noske, who was also responsible for coining the infamous slogan: 'Someone has to be the bloodhound.'[39] Even in the letters that he wrote in prison in July 1916 Liebknecht had realized that 'the chorus of hatred in every school' and the 'barbarically inflammatory speeches of a number of army commanders to their soldiers' had already unleashed 'an infernal orgy', the 'spirit' of which had 'produced the *Lusitania* atrocity'.[40]

Historians have failed to give an adequate explanation for the process of brutalization and for the mental contradictions that were found in German society during and after the First World War. Perhaps the most sensitive and, at the same time, the most disturbing analysis is Alfred Döblin's monumental *November 1918: A German Revolution*, a novel that runs to over 2,000 pages that was written in exile in America and that recalls Karl Kraus's 'The End of the World in Black Magic' in terms of its theme and methodology. Here Döblin views events from multiple perspectives in a way that invites comparisons with the modern cinema. He also draws on contemporary sources such as Berlin's newspapers. And yet the plot is overlain with 'dark radioactive rays'. The novel's main character gets no further with his questions 'as to where the horror of war, the incomprehensibility and shame of the years of murder originated and why, in the midst of life, a form of existence suddenly manifested itself of which all human beings must surely be ashamed'.[41]

CHAPTER 5

Criminals and Victims

The End of the *U-20*

The outrage felt by the opponents of the war, the storms of protest abroad and the exchange of diplomatic notes following the sinking of the *Lusitania* and other passenger liners had left the German commanders who were responsible for these actions profoundly unimpressed. Walther Schwieger, too, continued to perpetrate his murderous crimes off the Irish coast and in the North Sea. Only four months after sinking the *Lusitania*, he torpedoed an unarmed Canadian liner, the *Hesperian*, to the south-west of the Fastnet Lighthouse, although on this occasion, the passengers and crew were relatively fortunate and only thirty-two of them lost their lives. In the three days that followed, Schwieger sank another five vessels. On the first anniversary of his sinking of the *Lusitania*, he caught the White Star liner the *Cymbric* in his cross-hairs. Although there were no passengers on board, six members of her crew were killed.

The unscrupulous activities of German U-boats led the British Admiralty to commit acts that were likewise impossible to reconcile with the articles of international law and the conventions supposedly in force at this time. Above all, the Germans feared the deployment of Q-ships and U-boat traps, camouflaged warships that looked like ordinary merchant vessels but which carried concealed guns. Their aim was to tempt enemy U-boats into approaching and surfacing. When the latter were within firing range, the 'merchant vessel' would hoist the Royal Navy flag and attack the U-boat. The best-known attack of this kind, when the would-be culprits suddenly became the victims, was the sinking of the German U-boat, the *U-27*, by the British Q-ship, HMS *Baralong*, on 19 August 1915, when all twelve surviving members of the U-boat crew were shot while still in the water on the orders of the *Baralong*'s commander, Godfrey Herbert.

The British were equally ruthless when they later destroyed the U-boat harbours at Ostend and Zeebrugge. Prior to the attack, the German positions on the hill at Wijtschate close to the town of Messines had to be neutralized, and so nineteen landmines, each with an explosive force of twenty-one tons, were placed in tunnels beneath the positions and detonated on 7 June 1917. The force of the explosion was so great that thousands of German soldiers were blown to pieces, and it is said that the noise could be heard as far away as Dublin.

The final voyage of the *U-20* was less dramatic. After a joint action with the *U-30* in the Norwegian zone of operations, both submarines were returning home in thick fog when on 4 November 1916 they found themselves trapped on a sandbank off Bovsbjerg on the Danish coast. Like

William Turner, who had fatally chosen to steer the *Lusitania* towards the Old Head of Kinsale in order to gain his bearings, the two submarine captains hoped that a lighthouse would provide them with a navigational aid. But the Bovsbjerg Lighthouse proved an untrustworthy friend. Situated on Jutland's western coast, it, too, can tell a long tale of terrible shipping disasters graphically illustrated at the St George Strandingsmuseum. The insidious sandbanks have spelt the end of thousands of ships, notably two belonging to the British Navy, the *St George* and the *Defence*, which sank here in 1811. Only months before the *U-20* met its end here, the Battle of Jutland had been fought in the waters of the Skagerrak, the only major naval battle between the German ocean-going fleet and the British Grand Fleet. The new English warships – the much-feared Dreadnought class – proved vulnerable and the British sustained greater losses than the Germans, but the final outcome of the battle on 1 June 1916 was none the less indecisive. Over two days, 8,642 lives were lost without any appreciable change to the strategic outcome of the war. The Royal Navy was able to maintain its naval blockade, while the German fleet was forced to remain in harbour, leaving only its submarines to continue their devastating attacks.

The importance of the country's U-boats in terms of the German war effort is clear from the fact that Vice-Admiral Reinhard Scheer sent a small armada of battleships and large torpedo boats to the Danish coast in an attempt to salvage the *U-20* and the *U-30*. The *U-30* was refloated relatively quickly, but the *U-20* eventually had to be

1 The Old Head of Kinsale and its prominent lighthouse.

2 Memorial in Cobh recalling the victims of the *Lusitania* disaster.

3 British shipping companies traditionally dominated the transatlantic passenger routes. Cunard Line poster from 1875.

4 At the time of her maiden voyage on 7 September 1907, the *Lusitania* was the largest passenger liner in the world. Measuring 787 feet in length, she could accommodate 2,000 passengers and 850 crew members.

5 The interior of the *Lusitania* rivalled that of any luxury hotel. Contemporary illustration of the first-class dining room.

6 'My field is the world.' The German *Imperator* was not only a passenger liner designed for peacetime, but also a symbol of aggression.

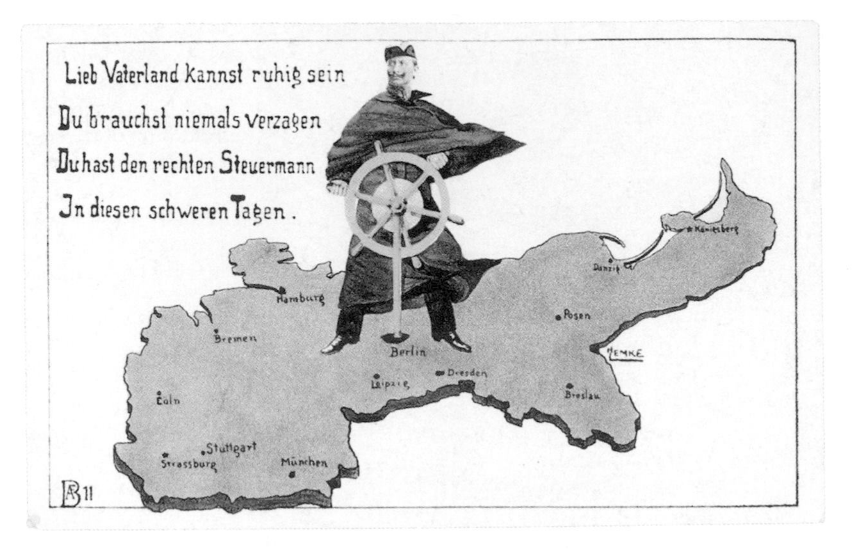

7 Kaiser Wilhelm II steering the ship of state. A postcard from the First World War. The caption reads: 'Dear Fatherland, you can rest at peace. / You never need despair. / You have the rightful steersman / In these difficult days.'

8 The new 'wonder weapon' was intended to bring about the longed-for change in the fortunes of war: German U-boats in Kiel harbour, 1914.

9 'The Submarine': an idealized depiction of submarine warfare from the *Illustrierte Kriegszeitung*.

10 A band of brothers: following their successes in the autumn of 1914, the crew of the *U-9* pose for a photograph in which they strike a heroic attitude.

11 Max Valentiner was famous as a U-boat commander and as the author of money-spinning adventure stories. Like most of his surviving comrades, he continued his career under the National Socialists.

12 The success of the submarine war was measured in tons: a German propaganda poster from 1918 indicating that, in the first half of 1918, Germany had built new vessels weighing 270,000 tons, while simultaneously sinking enemy ships weighing 630,000 tons.

13 The *U-9* under Captain Weddingen in convoy with other ships belonging to the German ocean-going fleet. Photograph from 1914.

14 Captain Walther Schwieger, the commander of the *U-20*. Following the sinking of the *Lusitania*, he was awarded the order Pour le Mérite.

15 Captain William Turner took command of the *Lusitania* in March 1915, only weeks before the vessel was sunk.

16 Advertisement placed in American newspapers by the German government warning against crossing the Atlantic in British ships.

17 Undated photograph showing the *Lusitania* crossing the Atlantic.

18 The *Lusitania* sank in only eighteen minutes. Irish poster, 1915.

19 Winsor McCay's animated documentary *The Sinking of the Lusitania* was intended to persuade the American public to declare war on Germany.

20 A contemporary cartoon from the *New York World* showing the ghosts of drowned children accusing the Kaiser of their murder.

21 Outrage at the sinking of the *Lusitania* led to the looting of German shops such as these in London.

22 'International law lies in the gutter, smashed to smithereens.' The Spartacus leader Karl Liebknecht (centre) and Rosa Luxemburg.

23 A German cartoon illustrating the claim that the *Lusitania* – here renamed the *Explositania* – was being used to transport munitions.

24 As First Lord of the Admiralty between 1911 and 1915, Winston Churchill was responsible for British naval policies.

25 An American army recruitment poster portraying the Germans as cultural barbarians.

26 The United States entered the war on 6 April 1917 under Woodrow Wilson.

27 A contemporary drawing equating the sinking of the *Lusitania* with the end of civilization.

28 A cartoon from the *Evening Sun*. Kaiser Wilhelm is seen bestowing an order on his bloodhound Walther Schwieger.

29 Thomas and Heinrich Mann are a prime example of the 'fratricidal war' between German 'culture' and western 'civilization'.

30 The First World War destroyed the avant-garde as an international network of artists. Cover illustration of the 1912 almanac of *Der Blaue Reiter.*

31 Picasso's *Guernica* (1937) remains a work of protest at the blurring of the boundaries of wartime violence.

abandoned, its final journey ending in a way that was pitiful rather than tragic. According to a reporter for the local *Holstebro Dagblad*, news that the *U-20* had run aground had spread like wildfire through the nearby town of Lemvig, where the locals 'barely found time to finish their breakfasts' before rushing down to the beach. Cars, motorbikes and bicycles blocked the road, and even the train that left the town at 9.30 that morning was almost completely full. It was around ten in the morning before the reporter reached the beach, where several hundred men, women and children were already gathered. They were speaking to the crew of a Danish lifeboat whose assistance the Germans had turned down.

The 'impressive' German submarine that had sunk the *Lusitania* lay only around thirty yards offshore, stranded helplessly on a sandbank. She was painted grey and moving only slightly in the waves that from time to time poured over her low foredeck, causing little white crests to form on the beach. The captain and his crew were standing together on the submarine and signalling to the rescue boats in an endeavour to reach an agreement. It was clear that all attempts to tow the submarine off the sandbank had failed and that the crew was preparing to abandon her. Explosive charges were set, and the crew was evacuated by lifeboats. Captain Schwieger and a companion remained on board until the end, lowering the German flag on the conning tower to half mast and then using a loudhailer to order the Danish spectators to take cover before they, too, climbed into a lifeboat. As the Danish reporter explained, there was a moment of drama when the explosives had already been lit and the engine on the lifeboat sputtered and died. Schwieger and his crew tried using wooden planks as substitute oars in order to row to safety. 'There was then an ear-splitting explosion, black smoke darkened the sky and pieces of metal from the exploding U-boat were hurled through the air.' The spectators who had sought refuge in the dunes were knocked over by the force of the blast or else they 'threw themselves face down into the marram grass'. By a miracle no one was hurt, and even Schwieger and his officer managed to reach safety in time.

Happy to have survived the explosion and clearly also pleased that the attempt to salvage the U-boat had failed, the onlookers streamed back to the beach and examined the wreck that remained on the sandbank. The whole of its front part had split into two, whereas its central section, including its conning tower and its stern had escaped almost entirely unscathed. 'There was only one man in the crowd who had reason to grieve over what had happened,' recalled the reporter. 'He was a German fish trader who happened to be staying in Lemvig. When the dynamite blew up part of the U-boat and the smoke enveloped the crippled vessel, he bared his head and murmured a few words, while tears were seen glistening in his eyes.'[1] A group of Danish women and children, by contrast, had themselves photographed on the wreck, their silent sense of triumph providing some scant compensation for the victims of the *Lusitania*.

The United States declared war on Germany on 6 April 1917. Captain Schwieger reacted very personally to this development, for the very next day he assumed command of the *U-88*, the newest and best equipped of all the German U-boats. For the next four months he patrolled the North Atlantic, indiscriminately sinking countless enemy and neutral vessels, including the British cruiser the *Hilary*, the Japanese passenger liner the *Miyazaki Maru* and another thirteen merchant vessels. The final voyage of the *U-88* ended on 5 September 1917 in a British minefield to the north of the Dutch island of Terschelling. There were no survivors. Among the victims was Schwieger.

The Turning Point of the War and Myths about the War

Even though the sinking of the *Lusitania* did not lead directly to the United States' entry into the First World War, Walther Schwieger created the political and psychological conditions for America's intervention when he fired his single torpedo at the Cunard liner. The harsh tone of the American protest notes already resembled an ultimatum. In its attempt to justify the incident, the German government sought 'to draw attention to the fact that the *Lusitania* was one of the largest and fastest English merchant vessels, that it was built as an auxiliary cruiser with government funds and that it appears in the Navy List drawn up by the British Admiralty'. The German government also knew 'from reliable information provided by its various departments and by neutral passengers that for some time past practically all of the more valuable English merchant vessels have been equipped with guns, munitions and other weapons and manned with personnel who are particularly adept at handling guns'. According to 'all the available information, the *Lusitania*, too, had guns on board when she left New York, guns that were kept hidden away below deck'.[2]

This was demonstrably incorrect. Although the *Lusitania* and her sister ship the *Mauretania* were on the Navy List as potential reserve auxiliary cruisers, the *Lusitania*, unlike the *Mauretania*, had never been refitted. It is clear from a search by the New York port authority that no guns had been installed, a point confirmed by all of the liner's survivors. Even the official report in the German Naval Archives for the naval war of 1914–18 concedes that 'The claim made by the German government and based on reports from the Admiralty Staff that the *Lusitania* was armed later turned out to be incorrect'.[3]

Conversely, there is no disputing the fact that among the *Lusitania*'s registered cargo were several thousand boxes of Remington rifle ammunition, empty shrapnel shells and non-explosive fuses that were deemed contraband under international law, and yet this does nothing to alter the fact that the sinking of the *Lusitania* contravened international law. Even if a part of its cargo contained 'contraband', unarmed merchant vessels could be sunk only if the ship had been warned in time and sufficient provision had been made for the safety of her passengers and crew.

German propaganda claimed, therefore, that a large liner like the *Lusitania* could never have been sunk so quickly with only a single torpedo: 'normally' passengers and crew would have had enough time to escape. The catastrophe, it was argued, was caused not by the torpedo but by the explosion of large quantities of explosives that were part of the liner's undeclared cargo. Ever since 1935, the year in which the wreck of the *Lusitania* was located, countless salvage expeditions have sought all possible causes for the second explosion but have never found evidence that there were explosives on board.

The most thorough search was undertaken in 1993 by a team of divers working with the marine archaeologist Robert D. Ballard, who established that the distance between the torpedo's point of impact and the cargo holds where unregistered explosives or volatile munitions would in theory have been stored was too great. Ballard is convinced that the second explosion was caused by coal dust that had become 'a highly volatile mixture force-fed with oxygen' resulting in 'a massive, uncontrollable explosion, a tidal wave of fire that rips through the ship's lower deck and blasts its way through the side of the hull'.[4]

According to one particular conspiracy theory that continues to enjoy a widespread following today, the British Admiralty under Winston Churchill deliberately steered the *Lusitania* into the path of the German U-boat's torpedo. As First Lord of the Admiralty, Churchill is said to have accepted the lives of American citizens as the price for persuading the United States to enter the war. This theory is based on a number of inconsistencies in British orders and actions. It is undoubtedly true that thanks to its secret operations base in Room 40 in the Old Building adjacent to

Horse Guards Parade, the Admiralty was in a position to decode the German Navy's radio transmissions and must have known about the *U-20*'s position prior to the disaster. Presumably Captain Turner did not receive this information and was never advised to change the liner's course. It has been impossible to establish whether this information was not passed on because the Admiralty failed to appreciate the importance of the messages that it had intercepted or whether its assessment was too riven by contradictions.

It is easier to answer the question of why the British cruiser, the *Juno*, which had been in the vicinity, did not protect the *Lusitania* but was ordered to return to Queenstown. Had the *Juno* been deployed to accompany and protect the liner, the latter would have forfeited the right to protection under international law: all vessels sailing in convoy could be sunk without warning. Moreover, the *Juno* was too old and slow and ill equipped to defend the *Lusitania* but would herself have provided any passing submarine with an excellent target in her own right.

The reactions to the tragedy on the part of the Admiralty do not support the view that Churchill had some 'diabolical' plot in mind. The director of the Naval Staff's Trade Division, Richard Webb, laid the blame at the door of the Cunard Line, alleging that the company had been infiltrated by 'German agents' who had obtained details of the *Lusitania*'s route.[5] Churchill himself and the First Sea Lord, Admiral Sir John ('Jackie') Fisher, both agreed that Turner had been guilty of 'almost inconceivable negligence'.[6] In the course of the official inquiries and legal proceedings that followed, the Admiralty's failings were ignored on the grounds of 'national security' and the judge, Lord Mersey, concluded that it was Schwieger and his superiors in Berlin who were to blame for 'one of the most unpardonable acts of the modern age'. Although Turner proved unskilled at defending himself, he was exonerated of all blame and remained in the service of the Cunard Company, who gave him command of a troopship, the *Ivernia*, in December 1916. This vessel, too, was sunk by the Germans off Cape Matapan in Greece on 1 January 1917, when thirty-six crew members and eighty-four troops were killed. Turner again escaped with his life.

The deliberate killing of civilians that began with the torpedoing of the *Lusitania* represented the breaking of a taboo which, combined with other events that unfolded in the spring and summer of 1915, not only influenced the way in which the war was conducted but more generally ushered in a complete change in the direction of the conflict. As the German writer Stefan Zweig noted in 1942, shortly before he took his own life while living in exile in Brazil,

> The moral conscience of the world had not yet become as tired or washed-out as it is today. [. . .] A violation such as Germany's invasion of neutral Belgium, which today [. . .] would hardly be complained of seriously, could then still arouse the world from end to end. The shooting of Edith Cavell and the torpedoing of the *Lusitania* were more harmful to Germany than a battle lost, thanks to the universal outburst of moral indignation.[7]

Germany and its allies found themselves under increasing moral and military pressure. The Triple Entente of Great Britain, France and Russia that had become a military alliance in 1914 was eventually joined by no fewer than eighteen new partners, including Italy, the United States, Portugal, Romania, Greece, Cuba, Brazil and China. Only Bulgaria threw in its lot with the Central Powers in October 1915. Italy's official entry into the war on 23 May 1915 was hailed by the fanatical nationalist Gabriele D'Annunzio as a valid response to German-Austrian 'barbarism', and in the pages of *Il messagero* he expressed the hope that the victims of the *Lusitania* had not died in vain but would prove 'useful' in persuading the Americans, too, to declare war on Germany. Long pent-up hatred found violent expression on the new front, which extended from the Swiss border to the Tyrol and from there along the Dolomites and Alps as far as the Adriatic. The fighting in the mountain regions turned out to be especially bloody and lasted until October 1918, chiefly in the region of the Isonzo and Piave rivers. As in the west, the front remained largely unchanged, a series of attacks and counterattacks leading to a stalemate, while days were spent preparing the artillery, the infantry tried to advance, cliffs were blown up and hand-to-hand fighting took place at altitudes of almost 13,000 feet.

In connection with the extension of the U-boat war in the Mediterranean, the Austrians drew up often absurd plans for the deployment of the new 'wonder weapon', and in August 1915 they even considered using a tiny submarine in Lake Garda to attack the steamships run by the

Italian customs authorities. The boat in question had been designed to research marine flora and fauna and was berthed at the port of Fiume. Less than 40 feet long and under 9 feet wide, it weighed forty-four tons and could reach a depth of 165 feet. It was additionally equipped with a porthole and an underwater camera. The Austrian Navy bought the boat for 200,000 crowns and refitted it for military use by adding a torpedo tube, installing a new engine and a periscope and making provision for a six-man crew. According to a detailed plan, the 'secret weapon' was to be transported by rail to Trento and then taken by road via Terlago and Vezzano through the Sarca Valley to Riva. To this end it was even decided to reinforce the bridge over the Etsch, but ultimately the plan came to nothing, no doubt because all of the resources on Lake Garda had to be concentrated on defending the Monte Brione near Riva.

Italy's self-appointed war hero Gabriele D'Annunzio would undoubtedly have relished a torpedo battle in Lake Garda. After the war he had the bow of the cruiser *Puglia* transported along the same route from the Mediterranean to Gardone, where it continues to grace the memorial to the Vittoriale degli Italiani – the 'Shrine of Italian Victories'. In general, the pre-Fascist belligerence shown in word and deed by D'Annunzio was not dissimilar to the battle frenzy of the German volunteers described by Thomas Mann in *The Magic Mountain*: 'They are a body of troops calculated as sufficient, even after great losses, to attack and carry a position and greet their triumph with a thousand-voiced huzza.'[8]

The acts of brutality increased exponentially with the use of poison gas on the western front followed by Zeppelin bombs dropped on London, by the carnage at Verdun, the famine in the east and the genocide in Armenia as the events of 1915 opened the gates to a hitherto unprecedented state of total war. Millions of soldiers and civilians were to lose their lives, several million more were left mutilated and traumatized. Even today it is impossible not to be appalled at the way in which this mass murder and deliberate self-harm was prayed for and acclaimed in millions of manifestos, essays, poems, novels, songs, paintings and sermons. All that we can say for certain is that no one sleepwalked his or her way into this nightmare.

A handful of observers such as Sigmund Freud had from an early date warned of impending barbarism. In August 1914, while Thomas Mann was looking forward to receiving 'good news from the battlefield' and 'from the field fortifications at Verdun, where honourable reality, true honour' was to be found,[9] Freud was writing to a friend about the 'wretched time' that 'this war' signified by 'making us too impoverished in both material goods and matters of the mind'. In 1915, in his essay 'Thoughts for the Times on War and Death', he sought to sum up his feelings of unease in the face of the war's upheavals:

> Then the war in which we had refused to believe broke out and it brought – disillusionment. Not only is it more bloody and more destructive than any war of other days,

> because of the enormously increased perfection of weapons of attack and defence; it is at least as cruel, as embittered, as implacable as any that has preceded it. It disregards all the restrictions known as International Law. [. . .] It tramples in blind fury on all that comes in its way, as though there were to be no future and no peace among men after it is over. It cuts all the common bonds between the contending peoples, and threatens to leave a legacy of embitterment that will make any renewal of those bonds impossible for a long time to come.[10]

Even before the war – notably in *Totem and Taboo* – Freud had examined those aspects of the denial of death that were bound up with national psychology. In 1915 he returned to this theme and described the change that had taken place in people's attitude to religious guilt. The biblical commandment 'Thou shalt not kill' had been extended to humankind in general, but in times of war the enemy was excluded from this injunction. The murderer now became the hero and was allowed to dispense with the complex rituals that primitive man had still had to perform in atoning for killing his enemies. The essay ends with a warning:

> To tolerate life remains, after all, the first duty of all living beings. Illusion becomes valueless if it makes this harder for us.
>
> We recall the old saying: *Si vis pacem, para bellum*. If you want to preserve peace, arm for war.

> It would be in keeping with the times to alter it: *Si vis vitam, para mortem*. If you want to endure life, prepare yourself for death.[11]

The sentiment Freud describes here as a kind of death wish on the part of all that then existed was reinterpreted by fanatical volunteers like Ernst Jünger as a wartime myth for young Germans. Only in the act of self-sacrifice could life truly find fulfilment even before it had been lived to the full, because in Jünger's view death was the meaning of life. From a literary point of view this message found arguably its most effective expression in Walter Flex's autobiographical novel *The Wanderer between Two Worlds*, which, first published in October 1916, had sold one million copies by the end of the war. Prior to 1914 Flex had been a private tutor for a number of aristocratic households, including Bismarck's, but on the outbreak of war he had volunteered to fight on the eastern front and by May 1915 had been promoted to the rank of lieutenant. His narrative tells of his experiences on the front with Ernst Wurche, a theology student and member of the Wandervogel movement until his death in August 1915. Flex himself was killed in action in Estonia two years later. His novel is like an Expressionist painting made up of homoerotic images, idealistic epic lays, *völkisch* nationalism, nature poetry and a longing for death, a mixture that was also to strike a chord with the National Socialists' youth movement.

Myths about the war were rife not only in Germany but in France, too, where Verdun became associated with a myth of a very special kind. Here the images associated with the town likewise reflected the horrors of war, but here there was no sense of yearning and no promise of redemption, for the French were not interested in revelling in the clash of arms or in invoking the horrors of materiel battles but only in protecting themselves from such horrors. Hence their idea for the Maginot Line, which stemmed not from a death wish but from the struggle for life. It was the French politician Georges Clemenceau who most clearly expressed his nation's desire to distance itself from the German myth of war:

> It is a part of human nature to love life. But the German does not acknowledge this cult. In the German soul, in German art and in the Germans' world of ideas and literature there is a lack of understanding of all that actually constitutes life, including its attractions and its greatness. In its place there is a morbid and satanic love of death. These people love death. These people have a god whom they view with awe but also with a smile of ecstasy as if overcome by dizziness. And this god is death. What is the reason for this? I have no answer to this question. The German loves war as a form of self-love and because a bloodbath awaits him at the end. The German welcomes that end as if it were his dearest friend.[12]

CHAPTER 6

'Malice in Kulturland'

In the battles fought by the wartime propagandists, the Germans were from the outset at a disadvantage, for they had been stigmatized as 'barbarians' and 'Huns' even after their first brutal violation of Belgian neutrality in August 1914. And after Germany's ruthless acceptance of so many civilian victims of the sinking of the *Lusitania* in May 1915, the English, French and Americans were finally convinced that the *furor teutonicus* no longer had anything in common with European civilization and morality. The French painted a crude picture of the Germans as the rabid *boche*, in England a pamphlet was published under the title *Malice in Kulturland* – the allusion to Lewis Carroll's *Alice in Wonderland* is unmistakable – and in America posters appeared depicting a fearsome King Kong figure wielding a club on which the word 'Kultur' was emblazoned, while magazines caricatured the German Kaiser as a military dictator. The New York *Evening Sun*, for example, published a cartoon showing Wilhelm II bestowing a military medal on Walther Schwieger as a reward for sinking the *Lusitania*, depicting him as a rabid dog, its jaws covered in blood.

The fact that the country's two most powerful generals, Hindenburg and Ludendorff, assumed control of the German war machine in the summer of 1916 was a reflection of the military and political crisis into which Germany had manoeuvred itself. Austria's position had been much weakened by the opening up of the new Italian front and this, coupled with the German navy's lack of success in the Battle of Jutland, the losses at Verdun and on the Somme, the unexpected Brusilov Offensive in the east and Romania's decision to side with the Triple Entente, meant that Germany had to reassess its war aims. While the political parties were apparently still arguing over the alternatives of peace through military victory or a negotiated settlement, Ludendorff, as the intellectual head of the army's supreme command, was already preparing the way for a military dictatorship. Wilhelm gave his approval to an authoritarian solution, leaving the chancellor, Theobald von Bethmann Hollweg, who was responsible for appointing his country's generals, reduced to the role of an impotent observer.

The most pressing question was that of the unrestricted U-boat war. In the face of vehement opposition and as a result of the war of words with the United States following the *Lusitania* disaster, the order to engage was temporarily limited, but by the end of 1915 the leaders of the army and navy had jointly demanded that the country's submarines be deployed without regard for the consequences as a 'flanking measure' designed to support the planned Verdun Offensive. With the support of the Admiralty Staff,

Ludendorff lost no time in insisting that the orders relating to the capture of enemy vessels be rescinded without delay, his aim being to ensure that Great Britain was defeated by German U-boats before the United States had a chance to intervene.

'Yesterday evening the chancellor said that the U-boats would pursue him to his grave,'[1] Bethmann Hollweg's adviser, Kurt Riezler, noted in his diary on 6 August 1916. Even before the war, Riezler – a classical scholar and philosopher by training – had exerted a considerable influence on the chancellor's policies, not least through his *Principles of International Politics in the Present Day*, which was published in late 1913 under the pseudonym 'J. J. Ruedorffer'. In general Riezler regarded war as the default mode in politics, a state interrupted by only brief periods of peace whose duration depended on the flexibility of the various alliances in force at any one time. In Riezler's view it was crucially important to resolve the tense situation between Prussia–Germany and Britain, a relationship he described as 'the most profound and most dangerous antagonism of our age'. In order to reduce the tension between the two powers, he argued, Germany's naval policies must be counterbalanced by some compensatory offer. For Riezler, it amounted to an act of suicidal madness to resume the country's brutal submarine warfare in the wake of the sinking of the *Lusitania*. In February 1916 he noted:

> Unrestricted submarine warfare is like an orgy of ruthless violence that fuels people's frenzy, leaving them feeling

> drunk. When you hear their shouts, it is almost as if the English are right to say that the Germans have gone mad. A drunken thrill at the use of violence. No one gives a thought to the fact that violence has limits and that everything depends on whether the use of violence is rewarded in terms of its overall consequences.[2]

It was with some reluctance that Bethmann Hollweg agreed on 9 January 1917 to the resumption of unrestricted submarine warfare, a weapon of war that would ostensibly help to decide the outcome of hostilities. Every attempt to mediate and sue for peace on the part of the recently re-elected Woodrow Wilson was in this way doomed to fail. Among large parts of the German population the propaganda accompanying the resumption of 'Viking raids' and their alleged 'success' had for a time the same effect as the reports that had circulated at the start of the war, in every case triggering a similar sense of euphoria. More level-headed observers such as Riezler were already sounding resigned:

> Worst of all is the U-boat question. If peace is restored this autumn, it will be far worse than people think, and the blame for this will be said to lie with the country's U-boats or, rather, with the refusal to deploy them. We shall have forfeited victory and lost our leading position in the world, and the troublemakers will apparently be proved right. Poor Germany will then fall into the hands of these people, half of whom are black marketeers, the other half fools.[3]

Riezler's diary entries chart the course of the internal struggle over Germany's war aims, and it is significant that the more moderate positions adopted by the Reichstag and by the German government quickly gave way to those of Ludendorff and the extreme right-wing 'national opposition' inside and outside the Reichstag. Ultimately all of them were at pains to establish an unequivocal German hegemony in Continental Europe as the precondition for German world domination. To achieve this end, the country needed, of course, to gain control of the seas, such fantasies reflecting the underlying imperialism of the German Reich and implying the hope that the existing conservative political and social system would be consolidated at home.

The 'hegemonists' not only enjoyed a majority in parliament but could also count on the support of influential figures in the world of German 'culture'. Whenever there was talk in the Reichstag of a 'negotiated peace', however cautiously that idea was raised, there were indignant protests in the country at large, nowhere more so than among its nationalist university teachers and intellectuals. In the summer of 1915, for example, the theologian Reinhold Seeberg collected more than 350 signatures from university teachers demanding a 'peace through military victory' that they advocated in response to the fear that 'a premature and ineffectual peace might be concluded on the basis of an illusory belief in reconciliation or even out of nervous impatience'. Such a peace, the petition went on, could not last and did not take account of the country's 'full international standing in a way that reflects the greatness of our cultural, economic and military power'.[4] When, in July 1917, the Reichstag passed a resolution by a large majority that included the Social Democrats, the Centre Party and the Progressive Party, all of whom were in favour of 'a negotiated peace and permanent reconciliation among nations' without 'any forced territorial acquisitions and political, economic or financial violations', their resolution was simply ignored by the military leadership, while more than one thousand university teachers signed a declaration that included the sentence:

> The undersigned German university teachers, unaffected by the views of any one party and free from special interests of every kind, but simply and solely motivated by their grave concern for the future of our fatherland, hereby declare their conviction that the present majority on the part of a Reichstag that was elected almost six years ago cannot claim to express the will of the people in any unambiguous way or to answer the vital questions that currently need to be addressed.[5]

'Nonpolitical Reflections' and the Germans' 'special path'

In 1914 the vast majority of Europeans had been enthusiastic about the war. Everywhere there were patriotic anthems and tears of chauvinistic emotion, but nowhere was the mood of jubilation as fervent as it was in Germany. On the day of universal conscription a crowd that had gathered outside the Berlin Schloss sang the Lutheran chorale 'Now Thank We All Our God', and the Kaiser, speaking from the balcony, announced that, 'If it comes to war, every party will cease to exist, we are now all German brothers.' The sense of universal solidarity gripped every social group, even though it was intellectuals, writers and artists who were best able to put into words the feeling of elation.

> What a man wants is what he hopes and believes. The overwhelming majority of the nation has long been weary of the eternally uncertain state of affairs. [...] The struggle of 1914 was not forced on the masses – no, by the living God – it was desired by the whole people. [...] To me those hours seemed like a release from the painful feelings of my youth. Even today I am not ashamed to say that, overpowered by tempestuous enthusiasm, I fell down on my knees and thanked Heaven from an overflowing heart for granting me the good fortune of being permitted to live at this time.[6]

The writer of these rhapsodic lines was the Austro-German 'artist' Adolf Hitler. A photograph shows him at a patriotic demonstration on the Odeonplatz in Munich on 2 August 1914, his features suffused with an expression of rapt transfiguration. During the first few days of the war there is no doubt that most Germans felt as he did.

One particularly striking feature of the Germans' enthusiasm for the war is its religious and philosophical component and the attempt to invest classical works such as

Goethe's *Faust* with a militaristic dimension. Intellectual sabres had been rattled with particular impatience during the relatively lengthy period of peace since the end of the Franco-Prussian War of 1870–71. The country, it was argued, needed to rearm. In 1891, for example, *The Military Faust* was published anonymously. Here the traditional enmity between the Archangel Michael and the Devil is trivialized by means of a series of carefully reworded quotations from Goethe's writings. As the patron saint of the Germans and the supreme commander of the heavenly hosts, the Archangel Michael was ranged against the no less well regulated troops of his fallen predecessor Lucifer. The graphic account of St Michael's protection and patronage and his role in Germany's fate was a popular element in the wartime propaganda that featured on postcards sent from the front.

These reductive versions of Goethe's *Faust* were effective only because the play – or at least Part One of the tragedy – was familiar to Germany's educated middle classes, while tens of thousands of copies found their way to the trenches. In March 1915 the Jena-based Frauen-Verlag published an edition of Part One in a miniature format as part of its German Fighters' Library, its preface aimed at those 'German fighters' who 'outside on the battlefield' were protecting their country and defending its honour. 'We women who have to remain behind at home can follow your feats only from afar, which is why the German poet should now be here for the German fighter.'[7] The Lilliput Library of the Leipzig firm of Schmidt & Günther likewise pressed Goethe into the service of the German war effort. No larger than a matchbox, its editions were bound in leather and protected by a slipcase. In 1915 the editor of the Goethe Society's yearbook, Hans Gerhard Gräf, was able to admire 'the knowledge of Goethe on the part of our doughty, broad-shouldered gunner'[8] who carried his copy of his 'Knapsack *Faust*' around with him in order to be able to work classical quotations into his letters from the front. Sermons delivered by army chaplains likewise combined the word of St Michael with Faustian revelations.

Patriotic poetry that was written during the war was no less riven by internal contradictions than the religious observation of the Germans at this time. The priests and pastors of the rival parties all declared the conflict a 'holy' war and blessed the use of weapons in a 'just' cause. During the materiel battles, Catholic army chaplains said Mass according to the same Latin rite, and Protestants, too, were indoctrinated into massacring their fellow Christians at camp services that followed a similar pattern. From August 1915 the Prussian Ministry of War even paid 'expenses' to army rabbis. Given their particular rivalries, the two major Churches in Germany sought to outdo one another in their professions of faith in Kaiser and country. By its very nature the Evangelical Church was closer to the throne and to the government than its Catholic counterpart since the Kaiserreich was grounded in Prussian national Protestantism. Its most influential propagandist was Bruno Doehring, the court chaplain and preacher in Berlin, who declared the Germans the chosen people, a people destined to save the world from the chaos caused by England's 'ruthless business sense', by France's 'blind hatred', Russia's 'ill-focused violence' and America's 'hare-brained mendaciousness'.[9] In August 1914 he had appealed to his fellow Germans to embark on a 'crusade', and in April 1917 he laid the foundations for the anti-Semitic legend that the Germans had been stabbed in the back: 'If Christ dwells within our nation, then they may murder us as the Jews once murdered our Lord, for a new Germany will rise up from our grave.'[10]

In word and deed, intellectuals, journalists, poets and theologians from all the countries involved in the war contributed in their various ways to their nations' spiritual mobilization. In both camps the war was portrayed as a struggle in which the very existence of the nation in question was at stake. The majority was in no doubt that it was the enemy that had started the war, and even writers who had hitherto been scrupulously fair no longer baulked at subordinating universal legal principles to the 'nation's right to life'. All observers were convinced that the war was necessary and that it would have a purifying effect not only on international relations but also on each nation as a community. And yet there were crucial differences between the different countries, for the process of politicization among the middle classes and the workers' movement had started much earlier in France and Great Britain than it had done in Germany. It was this contradiction, above all, that persuaded the educated elite in Germany to play its part in the war effort.

But did they know what kind of war they were cheering? Even those with long memories could look back on only two brief conflicts in the past sixty years, the Austro-Prussian

War of 1866 and the Franco-Prussian War of 1870–71: in each case a single battle had decided the course of the conflict after only a matter of weeks. In 1914, too, there were no plans for a long-drawn-out struggle lasting several years, and all the parties involved hoped that they would soon return home with the victor's palm. Social discontent as well as a delight in adventure had played a not insignificant role in motivating the different sides in the conflict. The long period of peace had produced a desire on the part of each of the warring nations to prove itself in the eyes of the others. A young and elite generation felt that their peaceful everyday lives were merely banal and they turned on a foreign civilization they felt was devoid of meaning, technically overcomplicated and clearly conditioned by material desires alone. 'We have branched out in too many directions,' complained Ernst Jünger:

> The sap no longer reaches the extremities. Only if an immediate impulse transfixes us like a lightning flash shall we again be simple and fulfilled, and this is as true of the individual as it is of the sum, the folk. It is on the tightrope walk between being and non-being that the true man reveals himself, for here his fragmentation becomes whole again, merging together in a few subversive activities of violent force. All the variety inherent in each and every form is reduced to a single meaning: battle.[11]

The Germans' actions threw a poor light on their cultural tradition, which now seemed to be logically connected to a policy of imperialist expansionism associated with the slogan 'Blood and Iron'. This reproach found its most extreme form in the writings of British authors such as J. W. Allen in *Germany and Europe* (1914), G. K. Chesterton in his essays and Joseph Conrad and Ford Madox Ford in their joint appeals and international campaigns. In France the philosopher Henri Bergson boosted the morale of his nation's troops with his bellicose lectures on the subject of 'intellectuality and freedom', leading to his election to the Académie Française in 1914 and his appointment to the post of Officier de la Légion d'honneur and Officier de l'Instruction publique. Another influential writer at this time was Émile Boutroux, whose polemical study *L'Allemagne et la guerre* was published in 1915. He had attended lectures at the University of Jena as recently as the summer of 1915, but turned away in disgust, so disillusioned was he by the German 'cultural barbarians'.

When the French pacifist Romain Rolland was retrospectively awarded the 1915 Nobel Prize for Literature, this was interpreted in Germany as a partisan declaration of support for 'civilization' in its conflict with 'barbarism', a clash of ideas summed up in the correspondence exchanged by Rolland and Gerhart Hauptmann following the German atrocities in the Belgian town of Louvain. The town was occupied without a struggle, but on the evening of 25 August shots were fired, killing several German soldiers. In an act of terrible retribution, the occupying Germans shot more than two hundred of the local inhabitants, destroyed more than a thousand houses in the historic centre of the town and burnt down the university library, with its holdings of 300,000 books and priceless manuscripts. Even more than the killing of civilians, it was the burning of books that caused outrage throughout the civilized world. 'Are you the descendant of Goethe or of Attila?' Rolland demanded an explanation from Hauptmann. 'Are you waging war on armies or on the human spirit?'[12]

The fact that well-regarded English and French philosophers and journalists accused Germany of 'barbarism' and, like Rolland, were honoured as a consequence was enough to infuriate many German intellectuals and academics, their fury finding expression in manifestos such as the appeal 'To the World of Culture' in October 1914. This appeal was organized by the writer Hermann Sudermann and signed by ninety-three prominent academics, artists and men of letters, including Gerhart Hauptmann and Max Planck. It also had the support of figures from the world of finance, representatives of the Foreign Ministry and the head of the news agency of the German Naval Office. In terms of its language and symbolism, the text took as its point of departure the Ninety-Five Theses of Martin Luther and was an attempt to refute the reproach that the Germans' actions in Belgium were an example of 'inhumanity', a charge dismissed as a 'blatant lie' and attributed to a 'conspiracy'. At the same time, the manifesto was designed to defend the good name of German militarism.

Each individual rebuttal of the charges levelled against the Germans was introduced by the inflammatory phrase 'It is not true'. It was 'not true', for example, that the life and property of a single Belgian citizen was violated by any of our soldiers unless the most extreme necessity required it, since time and again, in spite of all the warnings that were given, the local population persisted in ambushing our troops. The wounded were mutilated and doctors were murdered while performing acts of mercy. It is impossible to falsify the true facts of the matter in a more contemptible manner than by drawing a veil over the crimes of these assassins and interpreting the condign punishment that they suffered as a crime committed by the Germans. [. . .] Nor is it true that our military leaders have disregarded the provisions of International Law. They are innocent of any undisciplined cruelty. But in the east the blood of the women and children massacred by the Russian hordes stains the ground red, while in the west dum-dum bullets have ripped into the breasts of our warriors. Those who have joined forces with the Russians and Serbs and who present to the world the shameful spectacle of using Mongols and Blacks to hound white people have no right to set themselves up as the champions of European civilization. [. . .] Nor is it true that the struggle to defeat our so-called militarism is not also a struggle to overthrow our culture, as our enemies hypocritically claim. Without German militarism, German culture would long since have been wiped from the face of the earth. German militarism has emerged from German culture in order to protect it in a country that for centuries has been plagued like no other by pillaging raids. The

> German army and the German people are as one. This awareness now forges a brotherly bond between seventy million Germans without any distinction as to their education, social class and political party.

And the appeal ended with the words: 'Believe us! Believe us when we say that we shall fight this battle until it is over and that we shall fight as a cultured nation to whom the legacy of a Goethe, a Beethoven and a Kant is as sacrosanct as its hearth and soil. We vouch for this with our name and with our honour.'[13]

The appeal was published in all the leading German newspapers and triggered a range of reactions. Stefan Zweig, for example, knew from experience that in the First World War

> the word still had power. It had not yet been done to death by the organization of lies, by 'propaganda,' that people still considered the written word, they looked to it. Whereas in 1939 not a single pronouncement by any writer had the slightest effect either for good or evil [. . .] in 1914 a forty-eight line [*sic*] poem like Lissauer's 'Hymn of Hate,' an inane manifesto like that of the '93 German Intellectuals,' or an eight-page essay such as Rolland's *Au-dessus de la Mêlée*, or a novel like Barbusse's *Le Feu*, became an event.[14]

Ludendorff, too, was fully aware of the importance of propaganda for the conduct of the war and went to great personal lengths to ensure that when the Germans overran Liège, posters were displayed throughout the country hailing him as the 'hero of Liège'. Secret service studies were commissioned to investigate the ideological impact of British propaganda, while the cultural value of the still new medium of the cinema was recognized from an early date – in 1917 a central Photo and Film Office was established that was the forerunner of the UFA. In general Ludendorff took an active interest in making sure that 'ideas' such as those of the abovementioned appeal by the ninety-three intellectuals were disseminated as widely as possible as part of Germany's 'cultural mission'. In pursuing this aim he was able to rely conceptually and organizationally on the Pan-German League (Alldeutscher Verein) formed in 1891 as a protest at the Heligoland–Zanzibar Treaty that provided for the secession to Great Britain of Germany's colonies in East Africa. Its programme demanded more 'elbow room to safeguard those conditions that the Germanic race requires for the full deployment of its powers'.[15] The term '*alldeutsch*' was intended not only to extend the scope of the word '*reichsdeutsch*' but to define '*Deutschtum*' as a sense of patriotic loyalty.

Under the chairmanship of Heinrich Claß, the League adopted a more radical position with the outbreak of the war. Now it was no longer a question merely of combating France as the country's arch-enemy or of defeating its imperialist competitors Great Britain and Russia but of resisting Germany's internal enemies in the form, above all, of the Social Democrats and the Jews. In 1914 the League had still been a relatively small coterie with some 20,000 members, but its significance lay in its elite social representation: it had good connections with heavy industry and the larger aristocratic landowners – and two thirds of its members were teachers, journalists and officials working in the German education system, providing an excellent means of disseminating the 'ideas of 1914'. At the core of these ideas was the belief that the war would lead to the 'internal purification of the nation' and put an end to materialism and petty egoism. The war was to be invested with a Romantically nationalist dimension, according to which *Deutschtum* was defined as the opposite of French democracy (the 'ideas of 1789') and British liberalism, preserving and proving the distinctive qualities of 'German culture' in the face of 'western civilization'. After 1914 countless philosophers, sociologists, economists and writers were at pains to invest Germany's struggle with a hallowed goal and to surround it with a metaphysical aura of historical necessity. Among the most influential authors to pursue this goal of spiritual mobilization were the theologian and philosopher Ernst Troeltsch, the later Nobel Prize-winner Thomas Mann and the sociologist and economist Werner Sombart.

Ernst Troeltsch died in 1923 – he was fortunate not to have any direct contact with the rising tide of National Socialism. Modern commentators generally describe him as a philosopher of religion anxious to balance the competing claims of historicism and theology and of Church and State and as a figure rightly concerned about the future of European culture and keen to preserve the substance of

Christianity, while simultaneously wanting to be reconciled with intellectual modernism. And yet a number of his written and spoken remarks from the time of the First World War cannot be squared with this moderate view of him. On 2 August 1914, for example, Troeltsch, who had taught theology at the University of Heidelberg since 1894, called on his fellow Germans to take up arms. Like most academics, he was convinced that Germany was the innocent party in a war he regarded as a struggle for Germany's survival as a nation. His language was suitably bombastic: 'Our slogan rings out with all the magic of a virile, heroic mentality: to arms, to arms!'[16]

On 6 December 1914 Troeltsch addressed an audience of several thousand in the Municipal Hall in Karlsruhe, when he attempted to define 'the essence of the Germans'. The notion that European culture was a unified entity was a peacetime delusion, he explained, but that delusion had now been exposed for what it was. He distanced himself from France's historical concept of freedom and warned against the 'irrational and individualistic democracy' of the Anglo-Saxon nations. In particular, the 'democratic and Puritan idealism' of the Americans was dismissed as a form of instinctual arrogance that persuaded them to claim that their own political outlook and form of government were the only possible right ones. As a response to these contradictions, the Germans must 'immerse themselves in the depths of their own nature' and develop an 'unthinking resistance'. The strength of the German people lay in their 'monarchical' and 'military' character. Unlike the French, who were no more than 'a nation of pensioners', and the English, who as a nation were interested only 'in industry and trade', the Germans were 'an incredibly industrious people'. Germany, Troeltsch went on, had been forced to go to war by dint of the dynamics of labour and by the increase in the country's population. Now, as an empire 'striking out across the sea', Germany must pursue an 'oceanic' policy that would necessarily bring it into conflict with Britain.

As a theologian, Troeltsch was naturally keen to include the inner life of the Germans in his world view and to invest that inner life with a degree of stability that did not fight shy of clichés: if they were not to forfeit their souls, the Germans must ensure that their strict sense of duty and exceptional love of order were counterbalanced by an 'emotional life of great tenderness and refinement', by 'a sense of family and a love of our homeland, a love whose finest symbol is Christmas'. The German character, 'the German metaphysical and religious spirit' would therefore prove its superiority in war as well as in peace.[17] In October 1915, in a speech on the 'German idea of freedom', Troeltsch went on to appeal to the allied monarchies of Austria-Hungary and Turkey to assimilate the German principles of intellectual and spiritual order, for only then could the common 'cultural war' against those who were agitating on the world stage for 'the ideas of western democracy' ultimately prove successful. In this context Troeltsch clashed with Johann Plenge and Rudolf Kjellén, who between them had formulated the popular expression 'the ideas of 1914', insisting that while he had no wish to contradict the two sociologists, he wanted to 'lend depth' to their ideas, to which end he pointed out what he regarded as a 'certain similarity' between the events of the Napoleonic Wars of Liberation (the 'ideas of 1813') and the 'idealism of today'. It was the spirit of Kant, of Romanticism and of Goethe that had created 'a new form of Gospel' and the 'naturalness of the metaphysical belief in the divine and universal mission of *Deutschtum*'.[18]

The 'divine and universal mission of *Deutschtum*' was a high-flown way of referring to the desire to replace Great Britain on the throne of world dominion and offset the world of Romance ideas with the 'naturalness' of all things Germanic. In Troeltsch's view a group of decadent intellectuals had had a 'corrosive' and 'dispiriting' effect on this claim by dismissing 'all the moral and historical traditions' of German culture as 'sheer prejudice'. Above all, he was critical of those 'literary rodents' who in the face of war had 'disappeared into their holes in the ground' or 'preferred to strike a pseudo-patriotic note'.[19] Here is an example of the defamation of left-wing intellectuals combining with a form of anti-Semitic cynicism that found expression inter alia in the 'Jewish census' that was ordered in October 1916, a discriminatory measure designed to establish the number of Jews serving as frontline soldiers. When it turned out that German-Jewish frontline soldiers demonstrated an unexpectedly high level of willingness to sacrifice their lives and that there was none of the 'shirking' that the anti-Semites had supposed, the latter, sinking to new depths, accused the German Jews in question of 'ostentatiously pushing themselves forward'.

Following Bethmann Hollweg's resignation in July 1917, there were signs of a change of attitude on the part of patriotic academics who were no longer willing to place their unconditional trust in the dictatorial military policies of Ludendorff and Hindenburg. And when the recently founded People's League for Freedom and Fatherland held its first meeting the following January, the keynote speaker, Ernst Troeltsch, explicitly distanced himself from his earlier endorsement of his country's wartime propaganda and demanded a 'demobilization of the spirit', explaining that 'the war cannot be ended by purely military means' but only through 'the spirit of gentleness'.[20] This political change of heart naturally provoked mixed reactions, and while distinguished scholars such as the sociologist Max Weber, the theologian Adolf von Harnack and the historian Hans Delbrück supported Troeltsch's new desire to deplore the spirit of militarism, well-known writers such as Gerhart Hauptmann and Thomas Mann were not yet ready to embrace a demobilization of the spirit.

Thomas Mann in particular continued to express warmongering views. Since October 1915 he had been struggling to reformulate his ideas on the war in a new and more fundamental form in his *Reflections of a Nonpolitical Man*. That this project grew within three years to fill six hundred pages was due in no small part to the pressure on him to justify his views. Even in November 1914, when he had published his 'Thoughts in Wartime' in the *Neue*

Rundschau, he had interpreted 'German' culture and 'western' civilization as warring opposites. 'German militarism' was said to embody 'the form and phenomenon of German morality', while Germany's aggressive wartime policies were demanded by a 'moral imperative'.[21] Although remarks such as these earned him the approval of the Conservative camp, left-wing liberals both in Germany and abroad, including his brother Heinrich and Romain Rolland, were appalled.

'This is how the bull, maddened with rage, rushes into the arena with its head lowered, impaling itself on the blade that the matador holds out.'[22] Such was Rolland's comment on Thomas Mann's views, while his brother Heinrich attacked him personally in *Zola*, a plea for more civilized values that contains remarks such as this: 'Through their importunate attitudes, insanely arrogant nationalist poets, running with the pack and constantly firing off salvos, will for half a generation disclaim all responsibility for the mounting disaster.'[23] Heinrich Mann's *Zola* was a barely encoded confrontation with the other members of his family and, at the same time, a vengeful dismissal of Wilhelmine Germany that was prompted in part by the aftermath of the Dreyfus Affair in France. The author recalled that he too had 'once rebelled against the tyranny of patriotic incompetents who even in times of tranquillity were allowed to let off steam on certain stages'. But 'now, in more turbulent times, the whole country has become a chauvinistic fleapit'. 'National greatness' was limited to 'worshipping the sabre', and 'the intellectual fellow travellers' were 'more guilty than even the people in power'.[24] The intellectual controversy that was being conducted here, claiming that the Germans were following a 'special path' in pursuit of their teleological mission, was a continuation of a debate that had started in the nineteenth century. In his essays and novels, especially *Zola* and *The Man of Straw*, Heinrich Mann was critical of a misguided development in German history that was taking the country further and further away from the European example of modernism. Thomas Mann, conversely, was pleading for an alternative route, which he described as 'power-protected inwardness'. For him, the enemy was the 'political objectivism' of his brother.

But it was not just his private altercation with his brother that increased the pressure on Thomas Mann in the summer of 1915, persuading him to break off his work on *The Magic Mountain* and devote himself to a new polemical essay. In the wake of the *Lusitania* disaster he felt that as a would-be nationalist writer he was called upon to respond to the 'world-resounding hullabaloo that humanitarian hypocrisy had raised' following the 'sinking of the gigantic pleasure ship' that was an 'impudent symbol of English mastery of the sea and of a still comfortable civilization'.[25] His aim, in short, was to glorify his country's unrestricted submarine warfare as an expression of the German *Kulturkampf*. Decades later, in a letter that he wrote to Hermann Hesse on 8 February 1947, he sought to justify his 'nonpolitical' thoughts and feelings in 1915: 'The pacifism of political men of letters, of Expressionists and of the activists of that time got on my nerves, as did the propaganda concerning the Jacobin and Puritan virtues of the Entente powers, and

I championed instead a Protestant and Romantic *Deutschtum* that was apolitical and anti-political and which I regarded as fundamental to my whole way of life.'[26]

And so Mann spent the summer of 1917 working feverishly on the chapter 'On Virtue' in his *Reflections of a Nonpolitical Man*, while Ernst Troeltsch was calling for demobilization. In doing so, Mann launched a series of new intellectual offensives and forged holy alliances against the threat of a democratic levelling of German society. Luther and Goethe had long been on his side, he believed, but now he also had to enlist the help of Bismarck and Nietzsche as fellow combatants in his cultural war. He aimed to torpedo not only his brother Heinrich but humanitarian liberalism in general:

> I see and declare that what is now happening in Germany, that this process directed by civilization's literary man, who is preparing the intellectual capitulation of Germany and her integration into world democracy, is *reaction* – pardon the word, but it hits the mark – reaction against Nietzsche *and* Bismarck.[27]

This 'apparent self-contradiction' inherent in the meaning of the term 'liberal reaction' was 'the experience of our times, and it signifies essentially the "rehabilitation of virtue," the restoration and re-enthroning of the humanitarian-democratic ideology'. Mann was keen to prevent this, hence his appeal to the 'nonpolitical' path he believed the Germans must take:

> I do not want politics. I want objectivity, order and decency. [. . .] I myself confess that I am deeply convinced that the German people will never be able to love political democracy simply because they cannot love politics itself, and that the much decried 'authoritarian state' is and remains the one that is proper and becoming to the German people, and the one they basically want. [. . .] The difference between intellect and politics includes that of culture and civilization, of soul and society, of freedom and voting rights, of art and literature; and German tradition [*Deutschtum*] is culture, soul, freedom, art and *not* civilization, society, voting rights, and literature.[28]

Not until some years later was Mann able to accept a democratic republic as a political and intellectual form of order in keeping with the age, and it was not until 1922, in a sixtieth-birthday tribute to Gerhart Hauptmann, that he felt able to face the future and speak of a 'German republic'. And yet not even then was he prepared to admit that a German republic might have a 'civilizing' influence. And he imputed its birth not to Germany's defeat in 1918 but to the patriotic celebrations of August 1914: 'I dated the "Republic" not to 1918 but to 1914, to that time of new departures, when there was a readiness to confront death and when the "Republic" was created in the hearts of the nation's youth!'[29]

It was presumably Troeltsch's 1923 study on *Natural Right and Humanity in World Politics* that brought about a cautious shift in Mann's approach to 'civilization'. In his review of Troeltsch's book, he acknowledged the necessary connection between the traditions of the western and German ways of thinking. In what he termed an act of 'conscious self-correction' he now demanded a 'pedagogic' measure designed to ensure 'a rapprochement between the German way of thinking and those western European ideas that are inextricably bound up with certain religious and ideological elements in our culture group' – even if he did so 'while retaining the right to criticize the way in which the whole idea of anti-Christian humanitarianism has been allowed to rot and be misused for hypocritical ends'.[30]

In 1922, after years of ideological and political feuding, Thomas Mann had been reconciled with his by then seriously ill brother, and yet he was still unable to accept Heinrich's Francophile 'humanitarianism'. The enmity between the two brothers had survived the war, and the wounds were to take a long time to heal, a point that became clear when the publisher Samuel Fischer, planning to reissue the *Reflections of a Nonpolitical Man*, asked Thomas to remove a number of offensive remarks directed against his brother. Thomas wrote indignantly to his friend Ernst Bertram on 4 July 1921, announcing that 'Fischer insists on shortening the "Reflections" by between ten and twelve pages. Do you think that this is possible or even permissible?'[31]

Bertram, who had provided Mann with the ideas on Nietzsche he used in his *Reflections*, felt that cuts were indeed possible as long as the book's conceptual core, with its streak of Nietzschean Romanticism, was left intact. And so a shortened version of the book appeared in 1922, but Mann insisted that its 'nonpolitical' ideas had been preserved. 'I have recanted nothing,' he declared in his speech 'On the German Republic'. 'Nothing of any substance has been revoked.'[32] Above all, he shortened and rewrote those passages in which he had inveighed against his brother's 'glorification of Émile Zola'. And yet not even here did he recant his earlier views, for although the revised text appears to speak positively of Heinrich's 'political writing of the highest literary quality', it describes Zola in even more dismissive terms as 'an epic giant of animal sensuality, stinking extravagance, and filthy strength'.[33] And readers who might have expected that, four years after the end of the war, Thomas Mann would have been sufficiently self-critical to see that it would have been preferable to delete the passage celebrating the sinking of the *Lusitania* would have been disappointed. Here not a single word was removed or rewritten.

Thomas Mann remained bound by the thinking of Nietzsche as well as by the ideas of the economist Werner Sombart, whose 1915 pamphlet on the necessary rivalry between 'shopkeepers and heroes' continued to impress him. According to Sombart, the Germans as a nation of heroes felt committed to great feats and great ideas, whereas the British – and the Jews – embodied the shopkeeper's soulless spirit and the mean-spirited desire to make a profit. Mann, too, attributed these characteristics to the Anglo-Saxon world, characteristics that had traditionally been imputed to the Jews. And so in 1915 he was in full agreement with

Sombart's categorical conclusion: 'Rationalism is the basic feature of Judaism just as it is of capitalism.' For the nationalist economist as for the nationalist writer, it was clear that the battle line that had been drawn up was between a 'mercantile and a heroic view of the world and their corresponding cultures'. The present conflict was being waged as a 'war between nations over their respective view of the world'. The two nations who 'represent the two opposites' were the English and the Germans:

> And only as an Anglo-German war does the world war of 1914 acquire its deeper significance in terms of world history. But the important question that humankind must answer is not who will rule the waves. No, far more important and encompassing the whole of human destiny is the question as to which spirit will prove to be the stronger: the spirit of shop-keeping or the spirit of heroism.[34]

The philosopher Max Scheler likewise contributed to the debate in 1915 with his book *The Genius of War and the German War*, in which he proposed the view that the war was between the sublime German spirit and the 'perversity' of English civilization, a phobia that found its clearest expression in slogans such as 'Perfidious Albion! May God punish England!' and in Ernst Lissauer's aforementioned 'Hymn of Hate against England'. The classical scholar Ulrich von Wilamowitz-Moellendorff added his powerful voice to this chorus of disapproval. The then president of the Prussian Academy of Sciences and dean of the University of Berlin claimed that it was in England that 'the real driving force of evil that has summoned this war from Hell, the spirit of envy and the spirit of hypocrisy' was to be found:

> What do they not begrudge us? They want to undermine our freedom and our independence. They want to destroy that edifice of order, of civilized behaviour and of the freely self-assured freedom that we have constructed for ourselves and to destroy the excellence and order not only in our army and in our state superstructure but in our society as a whole. When the English naval officer looks through his fine and beautiful glass in search of German cruisers, he feels annoyed – and who can blame him? – that the glass was cut in Jena and that most of the cables that criss-cross the seas were made in Charlottenburg on the Nonnendamm. The sterling qualities of German workmanship rankle with him.[35]

How can we explain this hateful construct of an antithesis between Germany's 'self-assured freedom' and Anglo-Saxon 'hypocrisy', which found expression politically and militarily in the torpedoing of the *Lusitania* as well as in the witch-hunt against the 'inner England', in other words, against Social Democrats, left-wing politicians and Liberals? Was the ostensible 'self-assured freedom' not in fact a feeling of insecurity and 'envy' on the part of the Germans, feelings the latter were now imputing to the

British? Clearly there was a 'German angst' that had led to a feeling of aggression. Even the insane rivalry in building up a fleet of battleships had demonstrated that the Kaiser and the Wilhelmine elite vacillated between hatred and wonderment in their attitude to England. From a historical and psychological point of view, the situation was that of a family conflict that had escalated out of control. When, in his tirade against Britain, Wilamowitz-Moellendorff referred to 'self-assured freedom', he was thinking of the German version of 'mastery and servitude' described by Hegel and interpreted as the opposite of the western desire for freedom and equality. In his *Phenomenology of Spirit*, the voice of German idealism had proposed the social position of master and slave on the basis of their reciprocal recognition and awareness of the position of the other. The master owed his self-assurance to his power over 'the others', who for their part feared their master and submitted to him out of awe and identified with his self-assurance. The more powerful the master's position, the more impressively his light shone on his slaves, resulting in a 'harmony of inequality'.

Even before Karl Marx sought to turn Hegel's relationship on its head, the poet Friedrich Hölderlin had already shown great prescience in asking his philosopher friend: 'You see masters and servants, but not human beings – isn't that like a battlefield?'[36] But the battlefield was relocated. The master's self-assurance was declared to be a quintessential feature of the German character, and masters and servants found a suitable form of order in the German authoritarian state in order to defend themselves jointly against any change to the status quo. In this way the road that the Germans chose in their war on western democracy, equality and freedom acquired a metaphysical justification.

German Men of Letters

If the idea of segregating the 'German spirit' and divorcing it from the West assumed such fanatical and delusory forms, then this was due to the fact that it continued to be a highly contentious issue. In spite of all the differences between the cultural traditions that existed in Europe, the 'ideas of 1914' could not be fully equated with Kant's concept of the Enlightenment or with Hegel's philosophy of history as a German alternative to the French Revolution and to western civilization in general. Among the most violent objections to such a dichotomy are Heinrich Mann's three publications, *Zola* (1915), *The European* (1916) and *Kaiserreich and Republic* (1918), all three of which were reprinted in his anthology *Might and Man*, which serves as a kind of commentary on his novel *The Man of Straw*. 'Each in his or her own way,' we read at one point,

> we are moving towards a common goal – and not even our paths need to be separated for ever. Europe as a whole is in every one of us, all our different races are in each, each of them in all of them. There is not a single major region of ours that does not include an admixture of the basic racial types of the others. The admixtures

> differ, and depending on the demands of civilization and on historical conditions, one type or another will predominate in a particular region. In the past we Germans have occasionally desired a democracy in a way that few others have done, and yet we now believe in the right of the master in a way that no other does. We shall be forced to see the error of our ways.[37]

And he drew a distinction between the 'European vision' and the ideal of those crusading 'racist zealots' whose 'Teuton' was meant to look like 'an operatic Siegfried', even though he was in fact a mixture of Russians, Sicilians and Celts. 'Weak thinkers do not know themselves. They want to demonstrate the existence of a "Teuton", but what they describe is the European.' Heinrich Mann also recalled the close links between German poets and Anglo-Saxon cultural traditions, including in his list not only Goethe but also the early European Sturm und Drang writer Jakob Michael Lenz, who in 1775 had written a melancholic and effusive poem that he titled 'The Englishman'.

Mann's essay culminated in an impassioned plea for European unity:

> Even now the European enjoys freedom and self-determination as his inalienable right. But unity and internal peace are also his birthright. Our shared house has internal divisions that must be removed at some point in a better future. They must not be torn down by means of bloodshed. Nor must those who live behind

> them be destroyed. We know that this would be morally impossible; and since reason is the law that rules our lives it is also impossible in reality. A disaster, and then we continue. It may wound us but it cannot kill us, and it is bound to leave us feeling stronger. We are made to face disasters. Our war has not caused us to forget our deep conscience, a conscience known to the ultimate goal of our struggles. It is these struggles that shall lead us through the futility of our hatred to the unification of us all.[38]

Through his various writings Heinrich Mann came to be acknowledged as a proponent of the intellectual opposition to the war and of the peace movement whose members formed the nucleus of the Expressionist periodical *Die weißen Blätter*. Its editor was René Schickele, who as a pacifist and a Franco-German from Alsace found himself under attack and, following his outspoken criticism of the sinking of the *Lusitania*, became a person of interest in the eyes of the police, whose inquiries, as he himself observed, assumed 'excruciating forms'.[39] Like Leonhard Frank and other journalists, he was forced to move his offices to neutral Switzerland, a country to which many exiled men of letters owed their artistic survival after 1933 and which even during the First World War became a place of refuge for many opponents of the conflict who no longer had a homeland to call their own. In this way the country became the international centre of the pacifist movement. Here, too, Rosa Luxemburg's famous *Junius* pamphlet, in which the radical pacifist and social revolutionary demonstrated the links between the 'world drama' currently being played out on the battlefields of Europe and the current 'crisis in social democracy', was published in 1915 by the Zurich-based firm of Verlagsdruckerei Union. In 1916 and 1917 *Die weißen Blätter* was published first in Zurich and then in Berne.

Among the *Die weißen Blätter*'s German-speaking contributors were not only Heinrich Mann but also Hugo Ball, Eduard Bernstein, Martin Buber, Wilhelm Foerster, Hermann Hesse, Franz Kafka, Annette Kolb, Else Lasker-Schüler, Berthold Viertel and Franz Werfel. It was, however, remarkable for its international scope. The April 1915 issue was devoted to American literature and included a series of translations of poems by Walt Whitman collectively titled 'War'. After the journal's move to Switzerland, another issue was devoted to the French writer Henri Barbusse, excerpts from whose novel *Under Fire* appeared in a German translation. Published in France the previous year and presented in the form of a diary, the novel reworks the author's own experiences as a frontline soldier and is generally regarded as the first literary work to expose the mendaciously romantic view of war and to strike a more authentic note in describing the misery of trench warfare. Barbusse had volunteered in 1914 and served in the infantry, initially believing that war had a 'sacred' meaning, but he had soon become disillusioned and, filled with contempt, inveighed against the criminal military bureaucracy, the dull-witted enthusiasm of the press and the hypocrisy of the Church. But simple soldiers were invested with a genuine sense of humanity:

> They are not soldiers, they are men. They are not adventurers, or warriors, or made for human slaughter, neither butchers nor cattle. They are laborers and artisans whom one recognizes in their uniforms. They are civilians uprooted, and they are ready. They await the signal for death or murder; but you may see, looking at their faces between the vertical gleams of their bayonets, that they are simply men.[40]

In promoting his humanitarian message, Barbusse wrote what Heinrich Mann termed 'the most lasting chapbook' of the First World War,[41] but in the eyes of the militant representatives of the 'German spirit' it was inevitably a provocative text, not least because they had not yet forgotten his programme of 1914 in which he had advocated a 'socialist war' on 'militarism and imperialism, on the sabre, boot and crown, on the crown prince, on feudal masters and on lansquenets'. The world, Barbusse went on, could not free itself if it were not first liberated from these enemies. For Thomas Mann, there was an additional bone of contention in that the opening chapter of *Under Fire* appeared to preempt the underlying motif of his novel *The Magic Mountain*. In Barbusse's novel the horrific visions of the war are contrasted with the picturesque scenery of Mont Blanc, while the inmates of an elegant sanatorium half suspect the 'enormity' of the events that are taking place in the wider world and are afraid that the 'old world' is about to vanish for good. Even though *Under Fire* was much criticized by the nationalist press, by right-wing parties and by the reactionary clergy in France, Barbusse received the Prix Goncourt – his country's highest literary award – in the year of the novel's publication.

And there was a second French writer who in 1916 was acclaimed as a model for the international peace movement: Romain Rolland had been belatedly nominated for the previous year's Nobel Prize for Literature 'as a tribute to the lofty idealism of his literary production and to the sympathy and love of truth with which he has described different types of human beings'. He had already gained international recognition with his ten-volume novel *Jean-Christophe* of 1904–12, the hero of which is a German composer living in France and able to reconcile 'German resolve' and 'French intellectualism' through the medium of music. It was hailed as an expression of the need for greater understanding among nations and as an impassioned denunciation of the traditional view that the Germans and French were 'ancestral enemies'. Rolland was in Switzerland when the war broke out, and he decided to remain there and use the country's neutrality to champion peace. He donated his Nobel Prize money to the Red Cross and wrote a series of articles, 'Au-dessus de la mêlée', for the *Journal de Genève* that was reissued in book form in 1915.

From his position of intellectual dominance looking down on the warring parties, Rolland tried to win over both France and Germany and persuade them to agree to a negotiated peace. His activities were extraordinarily wide-ranging, since he was not only a journalist but also an organizer. Stefan Zweig visited him in Geneva and was overwhelmed by the aura that surrounded him:

> At last, then, I was in his room – almost it seemed to me to be the one in Paris. Here, too, stood the table and chair covered with books. Magazines, letters, and papers spilled from the writing table; the unpretentious, monastic working surroundings were the emanation of his very being, and were the same wherever he might be.

Zweig was

> fully aware that the friend with whom I stood face to face was the most important man of this crucial hour, that in him the moral conscience of Europe was speaking. It was only now that I could survey all that he was doing and had done in his magnificent service to mutual understanding. Working night and day, always alone, without help, without a secretary, he kept in touch with all efforts everywhere, conducted a vast correspondence with people who asked for advice in matters of conscience and wrote copiously in his diary every day; like none other in his time he was conscious of the responsibility of living in a historical epoch and he regarded it as a duty to leave a record for the future.

However, Rolland's health was much impaired. He could speak only very softly and invariably had to contend with a slight cough. He 'needed the protection of a shawl if he entered a corridor' and yet he was able to 'invoke powers which, under the strain of the claims made upon them, expanded unbelievably'.[42]

The French writer Pierre Mac Orlan struck a less moralistic and rather more ironical note when rejecting the view that the Germans were peculiarly conscious of their calling to travel the road to war and that culture and civilization were diametrically opposed to each other. His grotesquely polemic *U-713 or The Knights of Misfortune* of 1917 was superficially a parody of the Germans' enthusiasm for submarine warfare but was essentially a critique of the way in which human relationships and feelings had become mechanized. By 1916 English writers, too, had abandoned the earlier euphoria that characterized Rupert Brooke's 'The Soldier', for example. The new perception of war was embodied by younger poets such as Wilfred Owen, Robert Graves and Edmund Blunden, all of whom enlisted in the wake of the *Lusitania* disaster and, turning their backs on heroic stereotypes, came to regard the aestheticization of horror as mendacious. Traumatic experiences on the front persuaded Wilfred Owen to preface his collection of war poems with the statement that 'Above all I am not concerned with Poetry. My subject is War, and the pity of War. The Poetry is in the pity.'[43]

War Artists and Artists' Protests

The most radical artistic reaction to the war came from those painters and writers who founded the Cabaret Voltaire in Zurich in February 1916, when the idea of Dadaism was born. The movement's leaders were the poet and philosopher Hugo Ball; the cabaret artiste Emmy Hennings, whom Ball married in 1920; the writers Richard Huelsenbeck and Tristan Tzara; and the painters Hans Richter and Hans Arp. The Dadaists' anti-programme involved the destruction and denial of all traditional ideals and norms in art, culture and civilization, and it was in order to shed light on the meaningless nature of intellectual logic and bourgeois culture that Hans Arp added his surreal scribblings to the wordless sound poetry of Hugo Ball and Tristan Tzara.

But the authentic Dadaists were by no means unpolitical in their outlook. According to Arp, the massacres of the First World War were bound to induce a feeling of 'nausea caused by the foolish rational explanation of the world'.[44] This attitude also represented a rejection of the widespread tendency to see war as a form of art and as the representation of a higher form of existence. Not only the Italian futurist Filippo Tommaso Marinetti regarded war as a 'purifying force' and as the only way of cleansing the world,[45] but a number of German and Austrian avant-garde artists such as Otto Dix, Max Ernst, Ernst Ludwig Kirchner, Oskar Kokoschka, Wilhelm Lehmbruck and Franz Marc initially voiced similar views both as soldiers and as artists.

'My heart is not angry at the war,' Franz Marc wrote euphorically to Vassily Kandinsky in November 1914, 'but is profoundly grateful: there was no other transition to the times of the spirit, only in this way could the Augean Stables of old Europe be cleansed.'[46] The Expressionist *Blauer Reiter* group that Marc and Kandinsky had helped to found was disbanded, and Marc died in the trenches at Verdun in March 1916. The war destroyed not only individual artists' lives but also the avant-garde as an international cultural network. The Austrian painter and draughtsman Oskar Kokoschka likewise distanced himself from the Expressionist movement by evincing a marked enthusiasm for the war and in consequence was appointed an Imperial and Royal War Artist. As a volunteer in a crack regiment of dragoons he was seriously wounded in the Ukraine in the autumn of 1915, sustaining a bullet wound to his head and a bayonet injury to his chest, but he reported for duty again in the spring of 1916, taking part in the propaganda war on the Isonzo front.

The painter and draughtsman Max Beckmann evolved along very different lines as an artist, moving away from Impressionism towards Expressionism. On the outbreak of the war he declared that he would not shoot the French as he had learnt too much from them. Nor would he fire on the Russians, 'since Dostoevsky is my friend'.[47] As a result of his horrific experiences as a medical orderly on the eastern front and in Flanders he suffered a nervous breakdown in the summer of 1915 and was granted leave of absence. His breakdown led to a new beginning as an artist, and his sharply outlined drawings from this period document his complete departure from the figurative painting of the pre-war period. His images now depicted sad and helpless individuals, the wounded and the dying being shown in all their inconsolable wretchedness. *His Self-Portrait as a Nurse* and a cycle of lithographs titled *Hell* are good examples of the new, almost religious urgency of his style.

Arguably the most unusual anti-war protest to come under the heading of religious art was the work of the painter Friedrich Stummel, a body of work that continues to be the subject of church censorship. Stummel painted the apocalyptic figures of 'Pestilence', 'Death', 'War' and 'Famine' in a series of four scenes in St Mary's Basilica in the town of Kevelaer in North Rhine-Westphalia, concentrating on current suffering and on German war crimes. The images were painted on the wall in the south transept and centred around a reproachful representation of the sinking of the *Lusitania*, but other scenes depicted sieges and acts of destruction, including the German actions in Belgium and France. The injured were cared for by medical orderlies in neutral uniforms, and a soldier was seen sharing his bread ration with starving children.

By the summer of 1917 Stummel's frescoes had become a national concern following public criticism of their imagery. In its morning edition of 28 July, the *Kölnische Zeitung* published a piece by an unnamed 'lieutenant' who had been 'travelling through the famous place of pilgrimage' and discovered the offending frescoes during a visit to the church: 'It was a fresco of very recent date that left me feeling not a little appalled. In the south transept there is an image that is clearly intended to depict the horrors of war and the terrible effects of modern warfare.' But on closer inspection the lieutenant realized 'that the events depicted here are seen in a very one-sided way that leaves an unpleasant political aftertaste'. In the ruins depicted by Stummel, the observer believed he could see 'unequivocal allusions to certain buildings in Louvain' – the buildings in question were the town hall and library – and that the scene depicting a ship being torpedoed was an obvious reminder of the *Lusitania* disaster:

> Under the impact of a torpedo fired by a German submarine, a mighty ocean liner with four chimney-stacks is seen sinking beneath the waves. Observers may interpret these images as they will. I ask: is this pure chance? Or is it intentional on the artist's part? If it is chance, then we are dealing at the very least with a regrettable act of carelessness on the part of the Church's supervisory body, which presumably authorized the designs. But if the artist deliberately sought to conjure up the thoughts that force themselves on the observer, then he invites serious criticism on the part of every German who is fighting for his fatherland – and which of us does not number himself among these people at present?

The anonymous lieutenant also informed his readers that he had discussed the problem with a 'Catholic clergyman on whom the painting had left the same disagreeable impression'. And he felt obliged to stress that 'for a German it was certainly not a sign of a guilty conscience if he took exception to the scene that has been depicted here'.[48] This critical letter to the *Kölnische Zeitung* led to a debate between the church in Kevelaer and the episcopal see in Münster that was noted as far away as Berlin. When the government intervened, the bishop ordered the frescoes to be painted over.

Stummel had not previously attracted attention with his political views, making one wonder what had induced him to undertake this astonishing act of protest. His formal training and his earlier activities afford no evidence of a rebellious mentality. Friedrich Franz Maria Stummel was born in Münster on 20 March 1850. After attending his local cathedral school, he transferred to the Osnabrück grammar school, but left when he was sixteen without any formal qualifications. On discovering his gifts as an artist, he enrolled at the Düsseldorf Academy of Art, where for over a decade he was influenced by the Nazarene style of his teachers Ernst Deger and Eduard von Gebhardt. On completing his academic training, he travelled widely, visiting Italy and developing an interest in church interiors as a way of reviving the religious art of the Middle Ages. His first major commission were the frescoes in the chancel at Treviso Cathedral in 1878. In Rome he was introduced to the history painter Friedrich Geselschap, who in the early 1880s invited him to work on the Prussian Hall of Fame in the Arsenal in Berlin.

As a Nazarene, Stummel found it difficult to work on allegorical frescoes in praise of Prussian virtues, and it proved impossible for him to reconcile his understanding of religious art with the challenge of filling the vast surface inside the cupola, measuring 13 feet by 230 feet, with 'The Outbreak of War', 'The Subjugation of the Enemy' and 'The Crowning of the Triumphant Hero'. Stummel rejected the symbolism associated with the Prussian military and with the region's claims to power. Berlin, he felt, was a 'desolate wilderness', and so he returned to the Rhineland, with its spirit of contemplation. Although he completed a further commission in Berlin, designing the ornamentation in the Holy Rosary Basilica in Steglitz and in the Sacred Heart church in the district of Prenzlauer Berg, he turned down the chair of Medieval Painting at the Charlottenburg Academy of Fine Arts.

Kevelaer thus became Stummel's life's work after 1882, and although he accepted commissions in Aachen, Anholt, Cleves, Cologne and Luxembourg, he and his family settled in the town, where he built a huge studio and founded a School of Painting and Drawing. After years of preparatory work and with the help of a number of assistants, including Heinrich Holtmann and Josef Cürvers, he began painting the basilica in the summer of 1891. He continued to work on the chancel, the crossing and the south transept until 1912, but with the outbreak of the First World War he was no longer able to devote himself to it full-time. In spite of this the north transept was completed by 1916.

This was the year in which Kevelaer became a garrison and hospital town. The war-wounded were cared for in private quarters, and volunteers training to be deployed at the front had to attend edifying 'war sermons' in the basilica on Sundays. By now the wartime suffering had begun to affect daily life on the home front and to influence its rituals, and it was at this point that the Christian artist and his pupil Josef Cürvers decided to make a symbolic protest, resulting in the 'scandalous' depictions of the war the *Kölnische Zeitung* reported on in its edition of 28 July 1917, taking particular exception to the scene portraying the torpedoing of the *Lusitania*.

The scene in question was painted over shortly before the end of the war at the insistence of both the government in Berlin and the episcopal see in Münster. The protest and the resultant censorship were quickly forgotten, not least because there are no surviving photographs or sketches of the images in question. It was not until 1979 that the correspondence with the bishop was discovered in the Kevelaer Chaplaincy Archives and a description of the censored frescoes came to light. Today even these letters are locked away. When the late editor and publisher of the *Kevelaer Encyclopaedia*, Martin Willing, was researching an article on the subject at the end of 2011, he discovered that the relevant documents had been removed from the archival files. Willing's concern remains as topical as ever:

> Those of Stummel's war paintings that fell victim to censorship were the only ones in which the artist engaged in a critical debate with the here and now. Their loss is all the more painful in that they would have underscored the artistic significance of a man who is described as the 'last Nazarene' – and not always in a charitable sense. It would be worthwhile to examine the overpainted areas to establish whether the wartime images were actually destroyed or whether they still exist beneath the overpainted areas. If they still exist,

this group of Stummel's works could be restored to its original setting.[49]

It is no less true of the First World War in general that history is always viewed from the standpoint of the present. Our perception and assessment of historical events are as a rule coloured by national beliefs, and there are few interpretations that apply all over the world. The pictorial motifs of the German religious artist Friedrich Stummel are a major exception, reflecting, as they do, what could be called a European pattern of memory.

EPILOGUE

Delimitation and Continuity

By accepting a large number of civilian casualties as a result of the ruthless torpedoing of an unarmed passenger liner, the *Lusitania*, in May 1915, the crew of a German U-boat achieved the aim of 'total' war, a concept which, terrible in its symbolism, was later to be perfected by Erich Ludendorff. It involved what Golo Mann termed 'the elimination of the difference between civilians and soldiers'.[1] Within weeks a German Zeppelin had launched the first aerial attack on London, resulting for the most part in civilian casualties.

If we examine the deployment of U-boats, of bombs and of poison gas as well as the wholesale destruction of infrastructure and of rural areas and the Armenian genocide and see them as part of a wider picture, we shall have no difficulty in describing this phase of the First World War as a prelude to the Second. It marked the start of an industrialized erosion of the limits on violence that was to culminate in the horror of Auschwitz and in the destruction of cities such as Stalingrad and Hiroshima that were later to acquire symbolic significance. Studies undertaken by the Research Institute for Military History in Potsdam have described the 'delimitation of war' as a progressive 'social process' that influenced the 'social reality' of the different fronts as surely as it affected the 'struggle to interpret the experience of war' and the 'empirical reaction of foreign culture groups'. What is striking in terms of the course of both world wars is the finding that 'the inability to acknowledge the other side's sufferings and casualties' was especially pronounced in Germany.[2]

The First World War left seventeen million dead but brought no resolution to its manifold conflicts. The small new states that came into existence following the collapse of the old monarchies remained unstable, an instability fuelled by old and new resentments. After 1918 the various European powers failed to establish a new sense of balance among them, even though the October Revolution in Russia acquired transnational significance and for the first time in its history America now had a direct influence on the rest of the world. The United States first intervened militarily in Europe in 1917 and in doing so brought about a change in the fortunes of the war. And now that its soldiers lay buried in European soil, the United States believed that it had a right to have a say in future developments on the other side of the Atlantic. Its aims were peaceful. But when a new war broke out, the traditional alignment of powers was essentially repeated, with Germany ranged against Great Britain, France, Russia and the United States. As early as 1919 the French military leader Marshal Foch had predicted that the First World War would have a sequel. The Peace of Versailles, he argued, did not mean peace but only 'a truce' that would last twenty years at most. Although Germany's imperialist structures had been weakened by the country's military defeat and by the terms of the Treaty of Versailles, they had not been destroyed. Otherwise it is impossible to explain the rise of a new military power that twenty-five years later could overrun almost the whole of Europe.

A not insignificant role in this state of affairs was played by what the German historian Gerd Koenen has termed the 'unholy alliance' between Germany and Russia.[3] Even Lenin had sought a secret pact with the German Kaiserreich, and it was not just fear and horror that middle-class circles in Germany felt at the prospect of the Bolshevik revolution spreading westwards to their own country, for many Germans sensed a kind of cultural affinity with their neighbours to the east. Above all, Dostoevsky was compared to Nietzsche and hailed as a writer who had drawn attention to the soulless modernity of the West. Against this background, it was no accident that one of the early thinkers associated with the 'Conservative Revolution' in Germany, Arthur Moeller van den Bruck, had praised the 'Russian intellectuality' of Dostoevsky's writings.[4] In 1921 Thomas Mann characterized the relations between Germany and Russia as 'the comradeship between two great suffering peoples, both of which have a great future ahead of them'.[5] A particularly symbolic example of this self-contradictory 'alliance' was the fate of the famous Russian armoured cruiser, the *Aurora*, whose on-board cannon signalled the storming of the Tsar's Winter Palace in St Petersburg in October 1917: in September 1941 these same cannon were removed and used in the defence of the city which, by then known as Leningrad, was under attack from the Germans. The Hitler–Stalin Pact had run its course, and German aircraft sank the unarmed battleship while it lay at anchor in the city's harbour.

We can understand the epoch-making significance of the First World War only if we see it as the dialectic precursor of the Second World War. Only against this background can we understand why the First World War should so quickly come to be categorized as the 'seminal catastrophe' of the twentieth century, even if it remains true that the effectiveness of the expression rests on a misconception: historians were presumably able to agree on it so quickly because they left unanswered the question of guilt. And yet this is a question that is impossible to ignore for anyone taking a closer interest in the role and tradition of the various elites in both of these international conflicts.

For Golo Mann the Second World War may have revealed some 'entirely new characteristics', but in essence it remained a 'repeat' of its predecessor:

> The sense of repetition is everywhere, even on a personal level. Churchill and Roosevelt were already active during the First World War, only one or two rungs lower down on their respective career ladders. In 1942 Roosevelt not only repeated himself, he also repeated Woodrow Wilson, whose admiring friend and pupil he was. Roosevelt wanted to do better than Wilson and, wiser as a result of manifold experiences, to adopt a more realistic approach to the situation, but the basic conception

remained the same: in both cases the events that took place under their respective presidencies were seen as a struggle for democracy and the right to national self-determination in the face of autocracy and barbarism, culminating in the creation of a League of Nations and an ultimate end to wars of every kind. And yet – eerily – what was only partially true in 1917 and missed the essential point either hit the mark in 1942 or fell far short of that mark. In 1917 the world had cried 'Wolf!', although the Kaiser was really no threat at all. In 1942, conversely, the wolf was not only present but was far crueller than contemporaries realized. The American and Russian rivalry over how to win over the unfree part of the world and to gain the favours of a goddess of freedom who may or may not have been genuine had begun in 1917 and began all over again in 1941 but on neither occasion did it reach its climax until the war was over. Hitler's actions repeated those of the Kaiser and of Ludendorff, except that he wanted to do things far better than they had done. 'Then it was the Kaiser. Now it is I.' There is something altogether fateful about his dealings with Ludendorff, who even in 1916 had in his agitated and confused way already envisaged an end to the difference between civilians and soldiers. In his book on 'total war' and especially in his chapter on the military commander, he had offered a detailed description of the role that Hitler was later to assume, including Hitler's ultimate aperçu that the commander could be too great for his own people. After 1919 both men soon

> found themselves in agreement. What drove them apart once again was their differing views not so much on the matter itself but on the role that they themselves planned to play in the matter.[6]

Following his abdication at the end of the First World War, Wilhelm II lived in exile in the Netherlands, where he viewed Hitler's expansionist policies and anti-Semitism as a continuation and realization of his own particular goals. When German troops overran Paris in 1940 and forced France to capitulate, he sent Hitler a telegram, congratulating him on his achievements, and at the same time wrote to his sister, gleefully noting that 'The hand of God is creating a new world and working miracles. [. . .] We shall become the United States of Europe under German leadership, a united European continent, something that no one previously dared believe in.'[7] At a time when the SS leaders Heinrich Himmler and Reinhard Heydrich were already planning their 'final solution' and Anne Frank's family was attempting to hide in Amsterdam, the former Kaiser was striking a note of contented approval: 'The Jews are losing their baleful influence in every country and forfeiting positions that for centuries have led to feelings of hostility.'[8]

The German historian Friedrich Meinecke lived through both the Kaiserreich and the rise and fall of Hitler's Germany and was one of the first to recognize that elements of Hitler's belligerent expansionism and murderous anti-Semitism already existed under Wilhelm II, where they functioned as 'germ cells of the later disaster'. For him, the rise and fall of the two systems were part of a 'German catastrophe' whose 'initial storm clouds' had already darkened the skies of Europe at the end of the nineteenth century.[9] This is a question that has led to repeated arguments among German historians, notably in the early 1960s, when the Hamburg-based historian Fritz Fischer published his book *Griff nach der Weltmacht* – literally, 'Grasping for World Power', but published in the English-speaking world in 1968 as *Germany's Aims in the First World War*. In it, Fischer not only supported the view that Germany was largely to blame for the outbreak of the First World War but even argued that its political leaders had long planned the conflict as a war of conquest, the aims of which were barely distinguishable from those of Hitler himself.

Golo Mann's belief that the Second World War was a continuation of the first even on a personal level and that there was a sense in which history was repeating itself is particularly apparent in the area of German U-boat commanders, for, as we have already observed, almost all of the surviving submarine captains from the First World War held influential positions under National Socialism, the most striking example being Karl Dönitz, a submarine commander in the First World War who rose to the rank of commander-in-chief of the entire German U-boat fleet and German Navy in the Second World War. In May 1945 he was briefly Hitler's successor as his country's leader. His name is inextricably linked to the escalation of the naval war that was to lead to a number of appalling maritime disasters suffered by both sides in the conflict. These tragedies were deliberately engineered and began with the sinking of the *Lusitania* in May 1915. The catalogue of disasters includes the loss of the Soviet passenger liner, the *Armenia*, in the Black Sea on 7 November 1941, when more than five thousand wounded soldiers, civilians and refugees who were being evacuated from the Crimea lost their lives. The list also includes the 'Battle for the Atlantic' off America's eastern seaboard, when many thousands more were killed in 1942–43. In 1944–45 the conflict turned the Pacific and Indian Oceans into the graves of thousands of Japanese soldiers and civilians. And in 1945 thousands of German refugees drowned in the Baltic. On 30 January 1945 alone, the torpedoing of the *Wilhelm Gustloff* by a Soviet submarine resulted in the deaths of around nine thousand men, women and children, most of them civilian refugees from East Prussia.

From the outset Dönitz played an active role in revising and subverting the terms of the Treaty of Versailles. Initially the Germans were explicitly banned from possessing U-boats, but by 1922 the country had managed to build and test a number of new types of submarine using foreign contractors, including ones that were based in The Hague. And when the Anglo-German Naval Agreement was signed in 1935, allowing the German Navy to operate a maximum of seventy-two submarines, Dönitz insisted on taking full advantage of this provision, maintaining his position in the face of those who argued that the submarine was outdated as a military weapon.

By November and December 1936 – and in flagrant contravention of the articles of international law – German submarines were used in the Spanish Civil War, when a Republican submarine, the *C-3*, was sunk at the entrance to Malaga harbour. With the help of Operation Ursula, which was named after his daughter, Dönitz supported the activities of the German Condor Legion, which fought on the side of the insurgent General Franco. This was not just a question of 'Fascist solidarity' on an international level but, more generally, an attempt to try out new weapons and military tactics on behalf of the German Wehrmacht. On 26 April 1937, for example, the village of Guernica on the Bay of Biscay was subjected to an aerial bombardment by the Condor Legion that was supported by Italian aircraft. The attack lasted several hours and ended in the total destruction of the commune. Since there were no air-raid shelters or bunkers, the inhabitants were completely exposed to the hail of high-explosive bombs and firebombs. The attack amounted to a deliberate massacre of the civilian population and resulted in the deaths of 1,645 men, women and children. From a strategic point of view, Guernica was completely irrelevant but since the Middle Ages it had been regarded as a holy site in the Basque country, the focus of numerous religious and democratic traditions.

It was the Guernica massacre that persuaded Pablo Picasso to abandon his original project for the painting that he was preparing for the Spanish Pavilion at the World's Fair in Paris and that had been commissioned by the Spanish Republican government. Within a matter of only six weeks he had completed his world-famous canvas, a work of protest and mourning that occupies an area of over 300 square feet. Picasso did not depict the actual bombing of the town but the victims of the attack, brilliantly combining his Cubist surface design with religious iconography. The canvas depicts a space filled with dead and mutilated bodies, with a horse in the middle of the image and a bull on the left-hand side. A lamp hanging down from the top edge of the painting sheds its harsh light on the prostrate victims of the tragedy. In the foreground is a severed hand grasping a flower and a broken sword. The points of intersection of apparently arbitrary lines that are scattered across the whole canvas become so many explosive centres. The colours are almost entirely black, grey and white. Even now Picasso's *Guernica* retains its monitory force, regardless of the circumstances under which it was painted. Convinced that such a reminder was necessary, Picasso declared in December 1937 that 'artists who live and work with spiritual values cannot and should not remain indifferent to a conflict in which the highest values of humanity and civilization are at stake'.[10] His words were intended as a warning in the face of belligerent nationalism and as a rejoinder to Ernst Jünger's demand for 'total mobilization' and for the brain-washing of a new breed of cold-blooded 'men of violence'.[11]

In their discussions of the years between 1914 and 1945 historians, attempting to simplify the issue, have spoken of a new Thirty Years War. But such a comparison obscures the varying emotions that were felt when the two world wars broke out. In 1914 the great mass of people in Europe felt a very real sense of euphoria, but there could be no question of such an emotion in 1939. The continent's intellectual elites had a different awareness. It was not only the National Socialist bigwigs like Rosenberg and Goebbels who, responsible for culture, education and propaganda, wished to organize the 'battle for hearts and minds' in a better and more rigorous way than had been the case between 1914 and 1918; the same ambitions were shared by university teachers such as Paul Ritterbusch, who taught administrative and international law at the University of Kiel and who in the 1940s succeeded in mobilizing countless representatives of twelve humanistic disciplines, an initiative later known as the 'Ritterbusch Campaign'. A secondary aim was to create a new 'interdisciplinary' relationship with the natural sciences. While the humanities were to develop a suitable line in propaganda, the natural sciences were to provide the means to this end, the end in question being a continuation of the ideological battle fought chiefly between Germany and Great Britain. A unified peaceful order was to be established in Europe based not on western pluralism but on the 'inner, racial community and unity of the German people'. In Ritterbusch's words, it was the task of the new world order that was 'reborn from the National Socialist view of the world' to reveal the historical meaning of the new war and contribute to a 'coherent and conscious understanding and an intellectually clear attitude on the part of the German people'.[12]

Although National Socialism produced no unified political philosophy and although the start of the Second World War was marked by no 'ideas of 1939' comparable to the 'ideas of 1914' in spite of Martin Heidegger's attempt in May 1933 to revive those earlier ideas, the notion of the German *Sonderweg* – a 'special path' unique to the Germans – may be seen as a common thread. As early as 1917 the philosopher Ernst Krieck had attracted attention with his racist 'idea of a German state', and in 1940 he returned to the subject with a more far-reaching, anti-Semitic interpretation of a 'world idea of the German people'. Three years later the Tübingen philosopher Theodor Haering proposed an especially offensive definition of a particular brand of German domination:

> If the German spirit has nothing new to offer to others after this war and can provide them with nothing better than their nation's existing leaders and rulers, the meaning of this war, even after the greatest of outward victories, would remain questionable. In particular, those men and women who have recently spent time abroad have clearly felt that there, too, this question demands an answer because they genuinely expect something special of Germany.[13]

Whereas the leading thinkers of the Ritterbusch Campaign and the Rosenberg Office had been personally influenced by 'the ideas of 1914' while they were students and volunteer soldiers, the years after 1939 witnessed numerous intellectual initiatives on the part of younger scholars who had acquired their views on society under National Socialism. Some five hundred university teachers in the humanities were actively involved in the militant propaganda for a 'special' idea of German hegemony. The young scholar Hans Ernst Schneider, who after 1945 was able to continue his career as Hans Werner Schwerte, was particularly impassioned in his plea for the 'total wartime deployment of knowledge', seeing the radical delimitation of war as the task of German culture above all.[14]

Even during the First World War there had been calls for the humanities to be pressed into the service of the war effort. After 1939, German studies in particular developed a cultural terminology that was belligerent in the extreme. In July 1940 a conference of German teachers in Weimar had still been relatively vague in its reference to 'the possibility of a particular deployment in the war', but on 7 February 1943, writing in Goebbels' weekly *Das Reich*, Schneider proposed a more graphic definition in an article headed 'The Tragic and Stalingrad'. Against the background of the 'willingness to lay down their lives' of hundreds of thousands of German soldiers, the 'Nordic spirit's' capacity for tragedy was now invoked as a subject of academic enquiry. The 'Germanic and German myth' demanded that students of literature and men of letters forget their 'aesthetic yearnings' and acquire the 'resolute knowledge and the reality and the order that are a part of our blood'.[15]

As early as 1930, in his *Myth of the Twentieth Century*, Hitler's principal ideologue, Alfred Rosenberg, had already seen that Goethe's name was required to sanctify any National Socialist ideology since *Faust* was an expression of the Germans' very essence, 'the eternal element that dwells within our soul, assuming a new form each time that it is recast'.[16] The periods of elation in the Kaiserreich had made it possible for Goethe and his Faustian idea to live on and continue to be experienced, and even after the disaster of the Great War, Goethe was to be used in what Friedrich Ebert termed his country's 'transformation from imperialism to idealism and from a world power to intellectual greatness'.[17]

Even so, it required time and effort to ensure that Goethe and his contradictory oeuvre could be used directly for the purposes of National Socialist propaganda. Hitler's hostility to Weimar Classicism is well documented in the pages of Goebbels' diaries. In an entry for 1 February 1938, for example, the Führer is quoted as saying that 'Schiller and Goethe lived in a small regional capital and worked off their big ideas through the language of fustian'.[18] On the other hand, Hermann Rauschning records that in the light of Faust's line 'In the beginning was the deed', Hitler was 'prepared to forgive Goethe a lot',[19] and in 1939, Goebbels' Ministry of Propaganda, quoting the official party line, announced that Goethe was not 'an artist who lived and worked in a state of harmony', but, 'on the contrary, was invariably a fighter'.[20]

At those times in their history when the Germans' very existence has been under threat, Goethe's writings have clearly afforded a greater sense of consolation than other classics, and so the military reading of *Faust* enjoyed a revival. Faust's gesture of defiance in the face of destiny acquired particular significance after the 'decisive battle' of Stalingrad. The mood of disaster that was inspired by these events was captured by Theodor Plivier in his novel *Stalingrad*, which describes how the desperate Germans sought refuge in the 'hymnal' and 'leafed through Goethe's *Faust*'. As in the First World War, so in the second, copies of the 'Knapsack *Faust*' were declared the German Bible, and the programmes for every performance of *Faust* promoted the notion of the current conflict as a war of expansion – during the 1942–43 season alone, there were 310 productions of the play, and the actor and theatre administrator Gustaf Gründgens found himself constantly declaring that on the front line the 'idea of what has to be depicted' must be 'the idea of the soldierly'.[21]

In the occupied regions, too, it was one of the 'educational aims' of the SS organization Ahnenerbe (Ancestral Heritage) to promote German culture by means of Goethe. On 5 June 1941, for instance, one of the Secret Service's Situation Reports refers to a performance of *Urfaust* in Flemish as a 'special event' in the theatrical calendar. Such performances by visiting companies were said to 'strengthen the Flemings' sense of being a part of the Germanic community'.[22] During the final phase of the war Goethe's play was for the most part invoked whenever slogans were needed to appeal to the Germans' powers of endurance. Even warships were used as frontline theatres. In 1945, for example, Will Quadflieg declaimed scenes from *Faust* to an audience of marines on a

U-boat in the Baltic port of Neustadt. In his memoirs, he asked the rhetorical question: 'Reading Goethe to them was an extreme test even more than it was with other audiences. Could Goethe's language ever reach them?'[23]

In peacetime, too, Goethe could be cited in order to justify careers in every part of a country embarked on its 'special path' towards an absolute view of the world. This is especially true of the literary historian Hermann August Korff, who taught and published under four different systems between 1914 and 1957 without ever having to change his name or identity: the German Kaiserreich, the Weimar Republic, National Socialism and the German Democratic Republic. He served in the First World War as a lieutenant in a Hussar regiment. An external lecturer at the University of Frankfurt since 1914, he was appointed to a chair in German Studies at the University of Leipzig in 1923, retaining the post until 1954 in the face of the country's manifold political upheavals, allowing him to develop his underlying belief that only the 'spirit of the Age of Goethe' could save the West. The first volume of his four-volume magnum opus, *Der Geist der Goethezeit*, appeared in 1923, the last in 1953. In the 1930s, while German Jewish emigrants were alarming the American public with news of the National Socialists' reign of terror, Korff worked as a visiting professor in Harvard (1935) and Columbia (1938), willingly assuming the role of a Goethe specialist loyal to the National Socialist regime, permitting himself to be exploited for propagandist ends and to represent the 'official' German spirit. Not until August 1949 did he admit 'with the deepest sense of shame' that his 'faith in the Faustian individual – taken as a whole – had betrayed' him, but he clung to his old belief that 'We have no choice but to live and act as Faustian individuals! This is the law under which we reported for duty and under which Goethe, too, ends the final speech of his dying Faust.'[24]

National Socialism's official architect and later minister for armaments, Albert Speer, likewise refers to the symbolic significance of Faust in his memoirs, claiming that in Hitler he found his Mephistopheles: 'He seemed no less engaging than Goethe's.'[25] If National Socialism can be described as an 'efficient' organization, it owed this quality to the combined influence of the older and newer elites. More important than the role played by the Conservative and German Nationalist elites in Hitler's seizure of power and in his practical preparations for war was their role as intellectual leaders, a role that consisted for the most part in ensuring that anti-democratic and racist ideas became socially acceptable, but it was largely the 'new' elite that implemented them in the form of brutal policies.

Following the Kristallnacht pogrom on 9 November 1938, the American president, Franklin D. Roosevelt, expressed his incredulity that 'such things could happen in a twentieth-century civilization'.[26] Although the United States initially declared its intention of maintaining its neutrality in the Second World War, just as it had done a quarter of a century earlier, it supported Britain from the outset with weapons and war loans. And when Churchill and Roosevelt demonstratively spelt out their countries' shared values in the Atlantic Charter of August 1941, their declaration marked the beginning of a new cultural war. Following the Japanese attack on Pearl Harbor in November 1941, Hitler responded by personally declaring war on the 'degenerate' leadership of the United States, which was said to be as 'subverted by Jews' as Bolshevism. In the perception of British and American troops, too, battle lines were again drawn up between western civilization and German cultural barbarism, and the demon was again apostrophized as 'Malice in Kulturland', just as it had been in the wake of the *Lusitania* disaster.

As a result, targets often assumed a symbolic significance. And this was particularly true of the sinking of ships. In the case of the Rhine paddle-steamer, the *Goethe*, it was evidently its name that proved its undoing shortly before the end of the war. The ship had been launched in 1913 and was used to transport passengers and freight, but since September 1944 it was moored at Oberwinter, where it was used to accommodate several hundred forced labourers who were digging trenches on the Siegfried Line. Although the vessel was camouflaged and almost invisible beneath a high retaining wall on the left bank of the Rhine, it was specifically targeted by American low-flying bombers on the afternoon of 3 March 1945. Two bombs struck the stern and destroyed it completely. Twenty Russian labourers and the first mechanic were killed and numerous others were wounded, in some cases seriously.

No less symbolic was the destruction of Goethe's birthplace in Frankfurt in March 1944. Ernst Beutler, the director of the Goethe Museum, described the final tragic moments of this shrine to German culture as it was consumed by flames following an air raid on 22 March. The museum wing was burnt down at once, but the actual house in which Goethe had been born put up stubborn resistance. Although the attic was destroyed, the rest of the building as far as the second storey initially survived. Not until the evening of the 23rd did the stairwell cave in and not until the morning of the 24th did the whole building begin to lean from south to north, before 'collapsing with a clatter'.[27]

The whole country lay in ruins. A number of commentators wondered whether the end of the National Socialist system also spelt the end of the German concept of classical culture and education. It was clear that many leading politicians as well as military and cultural figures whose careers were irredeemably tainted continued to dominate their respective fields. In the course of the debate triggered by Daniel Jonah Goldhagen's *Hitler's Willing Executioners*, the journalist Frank Schirrmacher asked anxiously whether the Holocaust had been caused by 'Faustian striving'.[28]

The centenary of the outbreak of the First World War coincided with the seventy-fifth anniversary of the start of the Second World War. The German media were interested almost exclusively in the first of these international conflicts, memories of the second having been largely blacked out. It seemed as if no one wanted to see the historical links between them. The bestseller lists were dominated by books anxious to revisit the question of German guilt and to acquit the country of all responsibility for causing the First World

War, although historians such as John C. G. Röhl and Hans-Ulrich Wehler, repudiating the tendency to trivialize Germany's warmongers as men who 'sleepwalked' their way into the conflict, pointed out 'the massive German contribution to creating the fatal constellation that led to the war' and drew attention to the 'suppressed lines of continuity that extended until 1945'.[29]

Heinrich August Winkler, too, has reminded us that 'in no other constitutional state of the old West was political culture as marked by the tendency to think in militaristic categories as was Wilhelmine Germany'. In 1914 and, even more so, in 1918 the war had given rise to attempts to introduce a greater degree of democracy in many European states, 'but in scarcely any other country was the democratic new beginning as disadvantaged as it was in Germany'. In Winkler's view the debate over the crisis in July 1914 is fatally undermined by the fact that it largely excludes the question of the continuity between the two world wars. 'The effect of this has been disastrous. The revisionist view of the outbreak of the war encourages the tendency to adopt a nationally apologetic and, hence, uncritical understanding of German history.'[30]

For Hitler's biographer Volker Ullrich there is no doubt that the 'often strident German jubilation' at the theory that the Germans sleepwalked their way into war has a particular aim to it, namely, a 'historico-political attempt to change the course of German historiography. In the 1980s the Conservatives failed in their attempt to regain the high moral ground in interpreting German history, but this state of affairs was now to change.'[31] Significantly, the *Lusitania* tragedy has played no part in revisionist thinking, its symbolic significance and importance in terms of cultural politics having been comprehensively ignored.

And yet the point remains: no one slides uncontrollably into war. Wars are not accidently provoked by technology but are organized by human beings and prepared for by ideologues and by cultural and historical traditions.

Military conflicts continue to threaten world peace, yet history does not repeat itself in the manner of a blueprint. Even so, it is important to recognize that crises such as those in the Balkans, in the Ukraine, in Syria and in Iraq continue to be the long-term consequence of the collapse of old monarchies and other power structures. Today, religions leave their mark on national identities to a greater extent than nationalism once did. In Europe, former 'ancestral enemies' have become partners and even friends. The representatives and ideologues of the European Union claim that they have no wish to do away with nation states but are striving to achieve a political and economic union that is a force for peace on a global scale as well. Europe, however, is no mere 'text' or 'discourse' but a historical ensemble of harsh social and economic realities.

The 'normative project' of Europe and its transatlantic western orientation in the form of what Winkler has termed 'the quintessence of the ideas of the American and French Revolutions of 1776 and 1789 [. . .] needed two centuries to assert itself in the West'. This project, he argues, is 'cleverer than its creator' for its history has proved to be one 'of permanent self-correction and productive self-criticism'. It is a process, Winkler concludes, that is not yet complete.[32] The former German foreign minister, Joschka Fischer, takes a more sceptical view of this development and asks with some concern whether Europe will founder on its 'life-threatening crises', by which he means the internal 'crisis of sovereignty' and the external 'crisis of strategic security'. As a result, he fears the return of the two old demons of 'war and hegemony'. Of the two, he regards the internal crisis caused by Germany's new hegemonic role to be the more serious, for here we are dealing 'not with military or political ascendancy' but with the question whether Germany, as a 'European central power', will remain committed to its European mission and join forces with other countries to use its economic strength in support of European integration or whether it will see Europe only as a way of forcing through its own interests. Instead of pursuing the 'Europeanization of Germany', Fischer believes that politicians currently find it easier to envisage 'the idea of a German Europe'.[33]

If the plan for European integration were indeed to be thwarted by Germany, the result would be problematical not only from an economic perspective, but historically, culturally and democratically, too. Today the implementation of international rights and of transnational democracy seems more important than speculation on the international financial markets and military and technological rearmament. Germany must finally renounce the idea of a 'special path' and prove that it is a stable force in the western system of values capable of providing a feeling of solidarity. Then

Germany's intellectual elite will have a historic opportunity to work on behalf of a positive sense of continuity for the first time in its history. More than ever the new Europe needs the free and admonitory spirit of critical intellectuals for its humanitarian projects and designs. Such a spirit belongs to politics and society as surely as Mephistopheles does to Faust – and as surely as civilization belongs to culture.

Acknowledgements

This book would not have been written without the support and solidarity of Renate Lohse-Jasper, and it is she whom I must thank first and foremost. I am also grateful to Rüdiger Dammann and Axel Haase for discussing this project with me and for a number of ideas that have benefited this study and for their suggestions for improving the typescript. I owe a considerable debt of gratitude to Kirsten Hoffmann and Jürgen Karwelat for helping me in my research at the St George Strandingmuseum and for providing translations of foreign-language texts. The Military Archives that form part of the Federal Archives in Freiburg and the Newspaper Library at the Staatsbibliothek in Berlin were also kind enough to provide me with assistance. Tom Plunkett and Michael Martin were a fount of information that helped me to understand the historical background of the Old Head of Kinsale, the scene of many maritime disasters. Last but not least, I am grateful to Ulrich Hopp and Robert Zagalla for their editorial assistance.

Notes

Introduction

1. *Hamburger Fremdenblatt* (17 April 1912).
2. Quoted by Senan Molony, *Lusitania: An Irish Tragedy* (Douglas Village, Cork, 2004), 23.
3. Quoted by Wolfgang Zank, 'Hier große Freude . . .', *Die Zeit* (11 May 1990).
4. *Westfälische Tageszeitung* quoted in ibid.
5. Edwin Anderson Alderman quoted in Zank, 'Hier große Freude . . .' (note 3).
6. George F. Kennan, *The Decline of Bismarck's European Order: Franco-Russian Relations 1875–1890* (Cambridge, Mass., 1979), 3.

Chapter 1 · Report to Noah

1. Heinrich Gruner, 'Mittheilungen über die "Persia", das größte bis jetzt vollendete eiserne Dampfschiff', *Polytechnisches Journal*, cxl (1856), 1–14.
2. J. Kent Layton, *Lusitania: An Illustrated History* (Stroud, 2015), 91.
3. Robert D. Ballard and Spencer Dunmore, *Exploring the Lusitania: Probing the Mysteries of the Sinking that Changed History* (London, 1995).
4. Layton, *Lusitania* (note 2), 128.
5. Ibid., 145.
6. Hans Blumenberg, *Shipwreck with Spectator: Paradigm of a Metaphor for Existence*, trans. Steven Rendall (Cambridge, Mass., 1996), 10–11.
7. Edward S. Reaves, 'Lesson from the Tragedy of the Sea', *Baptist Courier* (2 May 1912) quoted by Steven Biel, *Down with the Old Canoe: A Cultural History of the Titanic Disaster* (New York, 2012), 243.
8. Stefan Gammelien, *Wilhelm II. und Schweden-Norwegen 1888–1905: Spielräume und Grenzen eines persönlichen Regiments* (Berlin, 2012), 389.
9. Thomas Mann, *Betrachtungen eines Unpolitischen*, ed. Hermann Kurzke (Frankfurt, 2009), 369; trans. Walter D. Morris as *Reflections of a Nonpolitical Man* (New York, 1983), 246.
10. Susanne Wiborg, 'Deutschlands "Titanic"', *Die Zeit* (8 April 1999).
11. Ibid.
12. Arthur Henry Rostron, *Home from the Sea* (London, 1931) reprinted in 2011 as *Titanic Hero: The Autobiography of Captain Rostron of the 'Carpathia'*, 155.

Chapter 2 · Modern Vikings?

1. Oswald Spengler, *The Decline of the West*, trans. Charles Francis Atkinson (London, 1971), 41.
2. Heinrich Mann, *Macht und Mensch: Essays* (Frankfurt, 1989), 184–5.
3. Max Valentiner, *Todesgefahr über uns – U 38 im Einsatz* (Munich, 2002), 68–9.
4. Quoted by Fernando Esposito, *Fascism, Aviation and Mythical Modernity*, trans. Patrick Camiller (New York, 2015), 163.
5. Valentiner, *Todesgefahr über uns* (note 3), 92–3.
6. Ibid., 94.
7. Lothar-Günther Buchheim, *Das Boot: Roman* (Munich, 1981), 162.
8. Promotional material on cover of Hans Steinuth, *England und der U-Boot-Krieg* (Stuttgart, 1915).
9. *Der Reichsanzeiger* (4 February 1915).
10. Valentiner, *Todesgefahr über uns* (note 3), 66–7.
11. Ibid., 77.
12. Ibid., 76.
13. Max Valentiner, *U 38 – Wikingerfahrten eines deutschen U-Bootes* (Berlin, 1934), 122.
14. Quoted by Wolfgang Zank, 'Hier große Freude . . .', *Die Zeit* (11 May 1990).
15. Dorothy Whitelock (ed.), *English Historical Documents*, i: *c.500–1042* (London, 1979), 842 (letter from Alcuin to Ethelred, king of Northumbria, after 8 June 793).

Chapter 3 · Minutes of a Disaster

1. Thomas Mann, *Betrachtungen eines Unpolitischen*, ed. Hermann Kurzke (Frankfurt, 2009), 369; trans. Walter D. Morris as *Reflections of a Nonpolitical Man* (New York, 1983), 246.
2. Quoted by Diana Preston, *Wilful Murder: The Sinking of the 'Lusitania'* (London, 2015), 72.
3. Quoted by Erik Larson, *Dead Wake: The Last Crossing of the 'Lusitania'* (London, 2015), 14.
4. According to John Protasio, *The Day the World Was Shocked: The 'Lusitania' Disaster and Its Influence on the Course of World War I* (Philadelphia, 2011), 213, the warning was published in six major New York newspapers and in no fewer than forty United States papers on 1 May 1915.
5. Quoted by J. Kent Layton, *Lusitania: An Illustrated History* (Stroud, 2015), 279.
6. Quoted by Larson, *Dead Wake* (note 3), 93.
7. Quoted by Des Hickey and Gus Smith, *Seven Days to Disaster: The Sinking of the 'Lusitania'* (London, 1981), 25.
8. Quoted by Susan Pedersen, 'Britain's Second Most Famous Nurse', *London Review of Books* (14 April 2011), 17–19.
9. Quoted by Sven Felix Kellerhof and Lars Broder Keil, *Gerüchte machen Geschichte* (Berlin, 2006), 57–8.
10. Georg Günter von Forstner, *Als U-Boots-Kommandant nach England* (Berlin, 1916), 18–19.

11. Quoted by Preston, *Wilful Murder* (note 2), 160.
12. Quoted by David Ramsay, *Lusitania: Saga and Myth* (New York, 2002), 67–8.
13. Quoted by Preston, *Wilful Murder* (note 2), 186.
14. Ibid., 189.
15. Quoted by Ramsay, *Lusitania* (note 12), 81.
16. 'Most Women Calm in Face of Death', *New York Times* (10 May 1915).
17. Quoted by Greg King and Penny Wilson, *Lusitania: Triumph, Tragedy, and the End of the Edwardian Age* (New York, 2015), 209.
18. Quoted by Robert D. Ballard and Spencer Dunmore, *Exploring the Lusitania: Probing the Mysteries of the Sinking that Changed History* (London, 1995), 105–8.
19. Preston, *Wilful Murder* (note 2), 252.
20. Quoted by Larson, *Dead Wake* (note 3), 283.
21. Ibid., 312.
22. Quoted in Ballard and Dunmore, *Exploring the Lusitania* (note 18), 115.
23. Charles E. Ives, *Memos*, ed. John Kirkpatrick (London, 1973), 92–3.

Chapter 4 · Jubilation and Horror

1. Quoted by Wolfgang Zank, 'Hier große Freude . . .', *Die Zeit* (11 May 1990).
2. Ibid.
3. Quoted by Diana Preston, *Wilful Murder: The Sinking of the 'Lusitania'* (London, 2015), 304–5.
4. Quoted by Greg King and Penny Wilson, *Lusitania: Triumph, Tragedy, and the End of the Edwardian Age* (New York, 2015), 254.
5. Quoted by John Protasio, *The Day the World Was Shocked: The 'Lusitania' Disaster and Its Influence on the Course of World War I* (Philadelphia, 2011), 134.
6. Quoted by Preston, *Wilful Murder* (note 3), 309.
7. Quoted by Des Hickey and Gus Smith, *Seven Days to Disaster: The Sinking of the 'Lusitania'* (London, 1981), 264.
8. Quoted by Preston, *Wilful Murder* (note 3), 307.
9. 'Lusitania', *Illustreret Tidende*, lvi (16 May 1915), 373.
10. Thomas Mann, *Betrachtungen eines Unpolitischen*, ed. Hermann Kurzke (Frankfurt, 2009), 369; trans. Walter D. Morris as *Reflections of a Nonpolitical Man* (New York, 1983), 246.
11. Ludwig Ganghofer, *Die Front im Osten* (Berlin, 1915) (20 May 1915).
12. Karl Kraus, *The Last Days of Mankind*, trans. Fred Bridgham and Edward Timms (London, 2015), 3.
13. Ibid., 547.
14. Karl Kraus, 'Tollers Publikum', *Die Weltbühne* (20 November 1919).
15. Kristina Schulz, *Die Schweiz und die literarischen Flüchtlinge (1933–1945)* (Berlin, 2012), 270.
16. Hermann Cohen, 'Deutschtum und Judentum (1915)', *Werke*, ed. Helmut Holzhey and Hartwig Wiedebach (Hildesheim, 1978–97), xvi.465–560.
17. Hans Mayer, *Ein Deutscher auf Widerruf: Erinnerungen I* (Frankfurt, 1988).
18. Erich Mühsam, *Tagebücher*, ed. Chris Hirte and Conrad Piens (Berlin, 2011—); online edition at www.muehsam-tagebuch.de (3/4 August 1914).

19. Ibid. (11 December 1914).
20. Ibid. (10 May 1915).
21. Ibid. (11 May 1915).
22. Ibid. (12 May 1915).
23. Ibid. (14 May 1915).
24. Ibid. (17 May 1915).
25. Ibid. (25 May 1915).
26. Ibid. (28 May 1915).
27. Ibid. (15 September 1915).
28. Ibid. (9 July 1915).
29. Ibid. (early February 1915).
30. Ibid. (25 June 1915).
31. Ibid. (4 January 1916).
32. Ibid. (29 March 1916).
33. Karl Liebknecht, *Ausgewählte Reden und Aufsätze* (Berlin, 1952), 296–301.
34. Ibid.
35. Karl Liebknecht, *Gesammelte Reden und Schriften*, 9 vols (Berlin, 1958–74), viii.318–19.
36. Ibid., viii.582 (letter of 15 April 1916).
37. Quoted from Mühsam, *Tagebücher* (note 18) (12 May 1916).
38. Liebknecht, *Gesammelte Reden* (note 35), ix.57.
39. Gustav Noske, *Von Kiel bis Kapp: Zur Geschichte der deutschen Revolution* (Berlin, 1920), 68.
40. Liebknecht, *Gesammelte Reden* (note 35), ix.89 (letter of July 1916).
41. Quoted by Jan Süselbeck, 'Der Teufel blieb aus' at www.literaturkritik.de (12 December 2008).

Chapter 5 · Criminals and Victims

1. *Holstebro Dagblad* (5 November 1916).
2. 'Deutschlands Antwort an Amerika', *Frankfurter Zeitung* (31 May 1915).
3. Quoted by Wolfgang Zank, 'Hier große Freude . . .', *Die Zeit* (11 May 1990).
4. Robert D. Ballard and Spencer Dunmore, *Exploring the Lusitania: Probing the Mysteries of the Sinking that Changed History* (London, 1995), 195.
5. Thomas A. Bailey and Paul B. Ryan, *The Lusitania Disaster: An Episode in Modern Warfare and Diplomacy* (London, 1975), 179.
6. Diana Preston, *Wilful Murder: The Sinking of the 'Lusitania'* (London, 2015), 314.
7. Stefan Zweig, *The World of Yesterday* (New York, 1943), 241.
8. Thomas Mann, *The Magic Mountain*, trans. H. T. Lowe-Porter (London, 1999), 714.
9. Thomas Mann, *Zeit-Echo*, i/2 (October 1914), 15.
10. Sigmund Freud, 'Thoughts for the Times on War and Death', *The Standard Edition of the Complete Psychological Works*, ed. James Strachey and others, 24 vols (London, 1952–74), xiv.273–302, esp. 278–9.
11. Ibid., 299–300.
12. Quoted by Christian Graf von Krockow, *Die Deutschen in ihrem Jahrhundert 1890–1990* (Reinbek, 1990), 99.

Chapter 6 · 'Malice in Kulturland'

1. Kurt Riezler, *Tagebücher, Aufsätze und Dokumente*, ed. Karl-Dietrich Erdmann (Göttingen, 1972), 371 (6 August 1916).
2. Ibid., 334–5 (22 February 1916).
3. Ibid., 361–2 (29 June 1916).
4. Quoted by Klaus Schwabe, *Wissenschaft und Kriegsmoral: Die deutschen Hochschullehrer und die politischen Grundlagen des Ersten Weltkrieges* (Göttingen, 1969), 69–71.
5. Ibid.
6. Adolf Hitler, *Mein Kampf*, trans. Ralph Manheim (London, 2002), 148.
7. Toni Schwabe (ed.), *Johann Wolfgang von Goethe: Der Tragödie Faust erster Teil. Erster Band der deutschen Kriegsbibliothek* (Jena, 1915), 5–6.
8. Hans Gerhard Gräf, 'Vorwort', *Jahrbuch der Goethe-Gesellschaft*, ii (1915), IX.
9. Quoted by Manfred Gailus, 'Bruno Doehring: Der Berliner Domprediger ruft den "heiligen" Krieg aus und erklärt die Deutschen zum Erlöservolk', *Die Zeit* (13 February 2014).
10. Ibid.
11. Ernst Jünger, *Der Kampf als inneres Erlebnis* (Berlin, 1922), 116.
12. Quoted in Anon., 'Furore Teutonico', *Der Spiegel* (21 March 1988), 259–61 (anonymous review of Wolfgang Schivelbusch's *Die Bibliothek von Löwen* [Munich and Vienna, 1988]).
13. Klaus Böhme (ed.), *Aufrufe und Reden deutscher Professoren im Ersten Weltkrieg* (Stuttgart, 1975), 47–9.
14. Stefan Zweig, *The World of Yesterday* (New York, 1943), 240–41.
15. Quoted by Rainer Hering, *Konstruierte Nation: Der Alldeutsche Verband 1890 bis 1939* (Hamburg, 2003), 121.
16. Ernst Troeltsch, *Nach Erklärung der Mobilmachung* (Heidelberg, 1914), 6.
17. Ernst Troeltsch, *Das Wesen der Deutschen* (Heidelberg, 1915), 16–17, 19, 22–6.
18. Ernst Troeltsch, 'Die deutsche Idee der Freiheit', *Neue Rundschau*, xxvii (1916), 50–75.
19. Quoted by Hans Liebeschütz and Arnold Paucker (eds), *Das Judentum in der deutschen Umwelt 1800–1850* (Tübingen, 1977), 99–100.
20. Ibid.
21. Thomas Mann, 'Gedanken im Kriege', *Essays II (1914–1926)* (Frankfurt, 2002), 27–46 (= Große kommentierte Frankfurter Ausgabe 15/1).
22. Romain Rolland, *Au-dessus de la mêlée* (Paris, 1915), 14.
23. Quoted by Klaus Harpprecht, 'Thomas und Heinrich Mann', *Die Zeit* (13 February 2014).
24. Heinrich Mann, *Macht und Mensch: Essays* (Frankfurt, 1989), 110–11.
25. Thomas Mann, *Betrachtungen eines Unpolitischen*, ed. Hermann Kurzke (Frankfurt, 2009), 369; trans. Walter D. Morris as *Reflections of a Nonpolitical Man* (New York, 1983), 246.
26. *Thomas Mann / Heinrich Mann: Briefwechsel 1900–1949*, ed. Hans Wysling (Frankfurt, 1984), XLVII–XLVIII (letter from Thomas Mann to Hermann Hesse, 8 February 1947).
27. Mann, *Betrachtungen* (note 25), 189; Engl. trans., 286.

28. Ibid., 33–5; Engl. trans., 16–17.
29. Thomas Mann, *Essays II: Für das neue Deutschland 1919–1925* (Frankfurt, 1993), 132–3.
30. Thomas Mann, *Aufsätze – Reden – Essays III (1919–1925)* (Berlin and Weimar, 1986), 428–31.
31. Ibid., 798 (letter of 4 July 1921).
32. Mann, *Essays II* (note 29), 132–3.
33. Mann, *Betrachtungen* (note 25), 206; Engl. trans., 135.
34. Werner Sombart, *Händler und Helden* (Munich and Leipzig, 1915), 3–6.
35. Quoted by Klaus Böhme, *Aufrufe und Reden deutscher Professoren im Ersten Weltkrieg* (Stuttgart, 1975), 59–60.
36. Friedrich Hölderlin, *Hyperion* (Weimar, 1921), 207.
37. Heinrich Mann, *Macht und Mensch* (note 24), 132.
38. Ibid., 133–4.
39. René Schickele quoted by Ahmet Arslan, *Das Exil vor dem Exil: Leben und Wirken deutscher Schriftsteller in der Schweiz während des Ersten Weltkrieges* (Marburg, 2004), 184.
40. Henri Barbusse, *Under Fire: The Story of a Squad*, trans. Fitzwater Wray (Charleston, n.d.), 211.
41. Heinrich Mann, *Ein Zeitalter wird besichtigt: Erinnerungen* (Frankfurt, 1988), 416.
42. Stefan Zweig, *The World of Yesterday* (New York, 1943), 265–6.
43. Wilfred Owen, draft preface for the collection of poems that was published in 1920; see Wilfred Owen, *Poems of War* (London, 1989), 7.
44. Quoted by Angèle Finck and Théodore Rieger, *A la découverte de Hans Arp* (Strasbourg, n.d.), 10.
45. Filippo Tommaso Marinetti, *Selected Writings*, ed. R. W. Flint (London, 1971), 42 (originally published in *Le Figaro* on 20 February 1909).
46. Klaus Lankheit (ed.), *Wassily Kandinsky / Franz Marc: Briefwechsel* (Munich, 1983), 265.
47. Max Beckmann quoted by Klaus von Beyme, *Das Zeitalter der Avantgarden: Kunst und Gesellschaften 1905–1955* (Munich, 2005), 577.
48. *Kölnische Zeitung* (28 July 1917).
49. Martin Willing, 'Stummel, Friedrich: Kevelaers bedeutender Künstler (1850–1919)', *Blattus Martini: Kevelaer Enzyklopädie* (online forum)

Epilogue: Delimitation and Continuity

1. Golo Mann, '1914 1939 Der Zweite Weltkrieg war die Wiederholung des Ersten', *Die Zeit* (14 August 1964).
2. Bruno Thoß and Hans-Erich Volkmann (eds), *Erster Weltkrieg – Zweiter Weltkrieg: Krieg, Kriegserlebnis, Kriegserfahrung in Deutschland 1914–1945* (Paderborn, 2002).
3. Gerd Koenen, *Unheilige Allianz: Rußland und Deutschland. Eine 400-jährige Faszination in Freundschaft und Feindschaft* (Frankfurt, 1990).
4. Arthur Moeller van den Bruck, Introduction to F. M. Dostojewski, *Sämtliche Werke* (Munich, 1922), i/1.V.
5. Thomas Mann, 'Russische Dichtergalerie', *Aufsätze – Reden – Essays III (1919–1925)* (Berlin and Weimar, 1986), 284.

6. Golo Mann, '1914 1939' (note 1).
7. Quoted by John C. G. Röhl, 'Kaiser Wilhelm II. und der deutsche Antisemitismus', *Vorurteil und Völkermord: Entwicklungslinien des Antisemitismus*, ed. Wolfgang Benz and Werner Bergmann (Freiburg, 1997), 285.
8. Ibid.
9. Friedrich Meinecke, *The German Catastrophe: Reflections and Recollections*, trans. Sidney B. Fay (Cambridge, Mass., 1950).
10. Werner Spies, *Kontinent Picasso* (Munich, 1988), 63–99.
11. Ernst Jünger, *Der Arbeiter* (Hamburg, 1932), 210.
12. Paul Ritterbusch, 'Hochschule und Wissenschaft im Kriege', *Kieler Blätter* (1940), 15.
13. Theodor Haering, *Die deutsche und die europäische Philosophie: Über die Grundlagen und die Art ihrer Beziehung* (Suttgart and Berlin, 1943), 25.
14. See Ludwig Jäger, *Seitenwechsel: Der Fall Schneider/Schwerte und die Diskretion der Germanistik* (Munich, 1998), 201–2.
15. Hans Ernst Schneider, 'Stalingrad und das Tragische', *Das Reich* (7 February 1943).
16. Alfred Rosenberg, *The Myth of the Twentieth Century*, trans. James B. Whisker (Newport Beach, 1982).
17. Friedrich Ebert, *Schriften, Aufzeichnungen, Reden II* (Dresden, 1926), 155.
18. Quoted by Ine van Linthout, *Das Buch in der nationalsozialistischen Propagandapolitik* (Berlin, 2012), 51.
19. Hermann Rauschning, *Hitler Speaks: A Series of Political Conversations with Adolf Hitler on his Real Aims* (London, 1939), 221.
20. Quoted by Linthout, *Das Buch* (note 18), 52–3.
21. Willi Jasper, *Faust und die Deutschen* (Berlin, 1998), 227–9.
22. Heinz Boberach (ed.). *Meldungen aus dem Reich: Die geheimen Lageberichte des Sicherheitsdienstes der SS 1938–1945* (Herrsching, 1984), vii.2370.
23. Will Quadflieg, *Wir spielen immer: Erinnerungen* (Frankfurt, 1976), 135–6.
24. Hermann August Korff, *Faustischer Glaube* (Leipzig, 1938).
25. Albert Speer, *Inside the Third Reich: Memoirs*, trans. Richard and Clara Winston (London, 1970), 31.
26. Franklin D. Roosevelt, press conference on 14 November 1938.
27. Quoted by Ulrike Eisenträger, *Material zum Projekt Wo Goethe wohnt: Zerstörung und Wiederaufbau* (Frankfurt, 2009), 23–4.
28. Frank Schirrmacher, 'Hitlers Code: Holocaust aus faustischem Streben? Daniel Jonah Goldhagens Remythisierung der Deutschen', *Frankfurter Allgemeine Zeitung* (15 April 1996).
29. Hans-Ulrich Wehler, 'Beginn einer neuen Epoche der Weltkriegsgeschichte', *Frankfurter Allgemeine Zeitung* (7 May 2014).
30. Heinrich August Winkler, 'Die Oktoberreform', *Frankfurter Allgemeine Zeitung* (1 June 2014).
31. Volker Ullrich, 'Nun schlittern sie wieder', *Die Zeit* (24 January 2014).
32. Heinrich August Winkler, 'Was nicht zerbricht', *Die Zeit* (1 October 2014).
33. Joschka Fischer, *Scheitert Europa?* (Cologne, 2014); see also Lisa Caspari, 'Joschka Fischer will Europa retten', *ZEIT-ONLINE* (14 October 2014).

Bibliography

Unpublished Sources

Cobh Heritage Centre, Eire
Department of Military Archives, Federal Archives, Freiburg
German Historical Museum, Berlin
Imperial War Museum, London
Lusitania Resource, The: History, Passengers, Crew, Biographies and Lusitania Facts (online archive)
Merseyside Maritime Museum, Liverpool
Newspaper Library, Staatsbibliothek Berlin
St George Strandingmuseum, Denmark
Staatsbibliothek Berlin, Digital Collections (1914–1918 War)
US National Archives and Records Administration (N.A.R.A.), College Park, Maryland

Historical Documents

Admiralstab der Marine (ed.). *Kriegstagebuch U-20: Kapitän Schwieger. Vom 18.3.15 bis 31.8.15*, vol. iii (Kriegsarchiv der Marine)
British and Foreign State Papers 1914–1917 (London, 1917–21), vols cvii–cxi
Buß, J. P. *Amerikanische Menschlichkeit im Lichte des diplomatischen Notenwechsels: Erste Veröffentlichung und Verarbeitung des gesamten deutsch-amerikanischen Notenwechsels* (Berlin, 1916) (= Kriegspolitische Einzelschriften, vol. xvi)
Liebknecht, Karl. *Der Hauptfeind steht im eigenen Land!* (May 1915)
Ludendorff, Erich von. *Urkunden der obersten Heeresleitung über ihre Tätigkeit 1916/18* (Berlin, 1920)
Niemeyer, Theodor and Strupp, Karl. *Die völkerrechtlichen Urkunden des Weltkrieges* (Berlin, 1920)
Steinuth, Hans. *Lusitania* (Stuttgart, 1915) (a comparison of the official German and American positions)

Historical Newspapers and Journals

Reports on naval policy before the First World War:
Denglers Polytechnisches Journal, cxl/1 (1856) (Cunard Line); and *Hamburger Fremdenblatt* (17 April 1912) (*Titanic*)

Reports on the *Lusitania* disaster from May to July 1915:
Berliner Tageblatt, *Chicago Tribune*, *Evening Sun* (New York), *Frankfurter Zeitung*, *Illustreret Tidende* (Copenhagen), *Minneapolis Journal*, *New Republic* (New York and Washington), *New York Herald*, *New York Times*, *The Outlook* (New York), *Vossische Zeitung*, *Westfälische Tageszeitung*
Foreign reports on the demonstration in Berlin on 1 May 1916:
Berner Tagwacht, *Daily Telegraph*, *L'Humanité*, *Nieuws van den Dag*, *La Domenica Illustrata*
Report on the stranding and scuttling of the *U-20* off the Danish coast in November 1916:
Holstebro Dagblad (Denmark) (5 November 1916)
Report on the artist's protest in the Kevelaer Pilgrimage Church:
Kölnische Zeitung (28 July 1917) and World War One: Centennial Gallery. The Great War as interpreted in magazine writings 1914–1918 (online presentation by J. Fred MacDonald)

Books and Articles on the *Lusitania*

Anon. 'The Lusitania Massacre – What Should America Do?', *The Outlook* (19 May 1915)
Bailey, Thomas A. and Ryan, Paul B. *The Lusitania Disaster: An Episode in Modern Warfare and Diplomacy* (New York and London, 1975)
Ballard, Robert D. and Dunmore, Spencer. *Exploring the Lusitania: Probing the Mysteries of the Sinking that Changed History* (London, 1995)
Ballard, Robert D. and Archbold, Rick. *Lost Liners* (London, 1997)
Ellis, Frederick D. *The Tragedy of the Lusitania* (Philadelphia, 1915)
Gentile, Gary. *The Lusitania Controversies*, 2 vols (Philadelphia, 1998–9)
Greenhill, Sam. 'Secret of the Lusitania: Arms find challenges Allied claims it was solely a passenger ship', *Daily Mail* (20 December 2008)
Grothe, Solveig. 'Der Untergang der "Lusitania": Angriff auf einen Mythos', *Spiegel-Online* (31 December 2008)
Hickey, Des and Smith, Gus. *Seven Days to Disaster: The Sinking of the 'Lusitania'* (London, 1981)
Historicus Junior [Albert Edward Henshel]. *The 'Lusitania' Case* (New York, 1915)
Hoehling, A. A. and Hoehling, Mary. *The Last Voyage of the Lusitania* (Lanham, 1991)
Kellerhof, Sven Felix. 'Die "Lusitania" war kein erlaubtes Ziel', *Die Welt* (26 June 2004)
Kellerhof, Sven Felix and Keil, Lars Broder. *Gerüchte machen Geschichte* (Berlin, 2006)
King, Greg and Wilson, Penny. *Lusitania: Triumph, Tragedy, and the End of the Edwardian Age* (New York, 2015)
Larson, Erik. *Dead Wake: The Last Crossing of the 'Lusitania'* (London, 2015)
Layton, J. Kent. *Lusitania: An Illustrated Biography* (Stroud, 2015)
Martin, Michael. *RMS Lusitania: It Wasn't & It Didn't* (Dublin, 2014)
Molony, Senan. *Lusitania: An Irish Tragedy* (Cork, 2004)
O'Sullivan, Patrick. *The Lusitania: Unravelling the Mysteries* (Wilton, 1998)
Preston, Diana. *Wilful Murder: The Sinking of the Lusitania* (London, 2015) ('Special Centenary Edition')

Protasio, John. *The Day the World Was Shocked: The 'Lusitania' Disaster and Its Influence on the Course of World War I* (Philadelphia and London, 2011)
Ramsay, David. *Lusitania: Saga and Myth* (New York, 2002)
Ripplinger, Stefan. 'Die Versenkung der "Lusitania": Über den U-Boot-Krieg 1915, einen deutschen Massenmord und ein Orchesterstück von Charles Ives', *Jungle World* (6 May 2010)
Sauder, Eric and Marschall, Ken. *R. M. S. 'Lusitania': Triumph of the Edwardian Age* (Chatham, 1993)
Simpson, Colin. *Lusitania: Special Merseyside Edition* (Higher Bebington, 1996)
Willing, Martin. 'Lusitania-Skandal: Zensur in der Marienbasilika Kevelaer. 1918 Kriegsbilder übermalt', *Blattus Martini: Kevelaer Enzyklopädie* (online forum founded in 1994 by Martin Willing and continued since 2014 by Delia Evers)
Zank, Wolfgang. 'Hier große Freude . . .', *Die Zeit* (11 May 1990)

Further Reading

Allen, William. *Germany and Europe* (London, 1914)
Angelow, Jürgen. *Der Weg in die Urkatastrophe* (Berlin, 2010)
Arslan, Ahmet. *Das Exil vor dem Exil: Leben und Wirken deutscher Schriftsteller in der Schweiz während des Ersten Weltkrieges* (Marburg, 2004), 184.
Assheuer, Thomas. '"Krieg veredelt den Menschen": Alles nur ein Spiel mit Worten? Thomas Manns berüchtigte "Betrachtungen eines Unpolitischen" in einer Neuausgabe', *Die Zeit* (4 March 2010)
Bajohr, Frank and others (eds). *Zivilization und Barbarei: Die widersprüchlichen Potentiale der Moderne* (Hamburg, 1991)
Ball, Hugo. *Die Flucht aus der Zeit* (Munich, 1927)
Barbusse, Henri. *Under Fire: The Story of a Squad*, trans. Fitzwater Wray (Charleston, n.d.)
Bayer, Martin and others. 'Erster Weltkrieg', *Aus Politik und Zeitgeschichte (Beilage zur Wochenzeitung Das Parlament)*, lxiv/16–17 (14 April 2014)
Becker, Jean-Jacques and Krumeich, Gerd. *Der große Krieg: Deutschland und Frankreich im Ersten Weltkrieg 1914–1918* (Essen, 2010)
Berghahn, Volker. *Europa im Zeitalter der Weltkriege: Die Entfesselung und Entgrenzung der Gewalt* (Frankfurt, 2002)
Bergson, Henri. *La signification de la guerre* (Paris, 1915)
Beßlich, Barbara. 'Wege in den Kulturkrieg: Zivilisationskrieg in Deutschland 1890–1914' (PhD diss., Darmstadt, 2000)
Beyme, Klaus von. *Das Zeitalter der Avantgarden: Kunst und Gesellschaften 1905–1955* (Munich, 2005)
Blumenberg, Hans. *Shipwreck with Spectator: Paradigm of a Metaphor for Existence*, trans. Steven Rendall (Cambridge, Mass.,1996)
Boberach, Heinz (ed.). *Meldungen aus dem Reich: Die geheimen Lageberichte des Sicherheitsdienstes der SS 1938–1947*, 17 vols (Herrsching, 1984)
Böhme, Klaus (ed.). *Aufrufe und Reden deutscher Professoren im Ersten Weltkrieg* (Stuttgart, 1975)
Bollenbeck, Georg. *Bildung und Kultur: Glanz und Elend eines deutschen Deutungsmusters* (Frankfurt and Leipzig, 1994)
Boutroux, Émile. *L'Allemagne et la guerre* (Paris and Nancy, 1915)
Brodbeck, David. *Defining Deutschtum* (New York, 2014)

Chesterton, G[ilbert] K[eith]. *The Barbarism of Berlin* (London and New York, 1914)
Churchill, Winston S. *The World Crisis*, 5 vols (London, 1923–31)
Clark, Christopher. *The Sleepwalkers: How Europe Went to War in 1914* (London, 2013)
Cohen, Hermann. 'Deutschtum und Judentum (1915)', *Werke*, ed. Helmut Holzhey and Hartwig Wiedebach (Hildesheim, 1978–97), xvi.465–560
D'Annunzio, Gabriele. *Contemplazione della morte* (Milan, 1912)
Dickie, Iain and others. *Techniques of Naval Warfare: 1190 BC – Present* (New York, 2009)
Döblin, Alfred. *November 1918: Eine deutsche Revolution*, 4 vols (Munich, 1995)
Doehring, Bruno. *Die Religion des Schlachtfeldes* (Berlin, 1916)
Döring, Jörg and Schütz, Erhard. *Benn als Reporter: 'Wie Miß Cavell erschossen wurde'* (Siegen, 2007)
Dunk, Hermann W. von. *Kulturgeschichte des 20. Jahrhunderts*, 2 vols (Munich 2004)
Ebert, Friedrich. *Schriften, Aufzeichnungen, Reden*, 2 vols (Dresden, 1926)
Eisenträger, Ulrike. *Material zum Projekt Wo Goethe wohnt: Zerstörung und Wiederaufbau* (Frankfurt, 2009)
Eksteins, Modris. *Tanz über Gräben: Die Geburt der Moderne und der Erste Weltkrieg* (Reinbek, 1990)
Elias, Norbert. *Über den Prozess der Zivilisation*, 2 vols (Frankfurt, 1997)
Enzensberger, Hans Magnus. *The Sinking of the 'Titanic'* (Manchester, 1981)
Esposito, Fernando. *Fascism, Aviation and Mythical Modernity* (New York, 2015)
Finck, Angèle and Rieger, Théodore. *A la découverte de Hans Arp* (Strasbourg, n.d.)
Fischer, Fritz. *Germany's Aims in the First World War*, trans. Hajo Holborn and James Joll (New York, 1968)
——. *From Kaiserreich to the Third Reich: Elements of Continuity in German History*, trans. Roger Fletcher (London, 1986)
Fischer, Joschka. *Scheitert Europa?* (Cologne, 2014)
Fisher, Admiral Lord John. *Memories* (London, 1915)
Flasch, Kurt. *Die geistige Mobilmachung: Die deutschen Intellektuellen und der Erste Weltkrieg. Ein Versuch* (Berlin, 2000)
Forstner, Georg Günter von. *Als U-Boots-Kommandant nach England* (Berlin, 1916)
Fossgreen, Anke. 'Auf der Titanic wurde gesungen, auf der Lusitania gekämpft', *Tages-Anzeiger* (5 March 2010)
Frank, Leonhard. *Der Mensch ist gut* (Zurich, 1917)
Freud, Sigmund. *The Standard Edition of the Complete Psychological Works*, ed. James Strachey and others, 24 vols (London, 1953–74)
Frost, Wesley. *German Submarine Warfare* (London, 1918)
Geiss, Imanuel. *Das deutsche Reich und der Erste Weltkrieg* (Munich and Zurich, 1985)
Glaser, Hermann. *Kleine Kulturgeschichte Deutschlands im 20. Jahrhundert* (Munich, 2002)
Goldhagen, Daniel Jonah. *Hitler's Willing Executioners: Ordinary Germans and the Holocaust* (New York, 1996)

Gräf, Hans Gerhard. 'Vorwort', *Jahrbuch der Goethe-Gesellschaft*, ii (1915), V–XII
Gut, Philipp. *Thomas Manns Idee einer Deutschen Kultur* (Frankfurt, 2008)
Haering, Theodor. *Die deutsche und die europäische Philosophie: Über die Grundlagen und die Art ihrer Beziehung* (Stuttgart and Berlin, 1943)
Hansen, Erik Fosnes. *Psalm at Journey's End* (London, 1997)
Hering, Rainer. *Konstruierte Nation: Der Alldeutsche Verband 1890 bis 1939* (Hamburg, 2003)
Hirschfeld, Gerhard. 'Erster Weltkrieg–Zweiter Weltkrieg: Kriegserfahrungen in Deutschland. Neuere Ansätze und Überlegungen zu einem diachronen Vergleich', *Zeitgeschichte-online. Thema: Fronterlebnis und Nachkriegsordnung, Wirkung und Wahrnehmung des Ersten Weltkriegs* (May 2004)
—— and others. *'Keiner fühlt sich hier mehr als Mensch . . . .' Erlebnis und Wirkung des Ersten Weltkriegs* (Essen, 1993)
Hoeres, Peter. *Der Krieg der Philosophen: Die deutsche und britische Philosophie im Ersten Weltkrieg* (Paderborn, 2004)
Horne, John and Kramer, Alan. *German Atrocities, 1914: A History of Denial* (New Haven, 2001)
Howard, Michael. *War in European History* (Oxford, 2009)
Huck, Stephan (ed.). *100 Jahre U-Boote in deutschen Marinen: Ereignisse – Technik – Mentalitäten – Rezeption* (Bochum, 2011)
Huntington, Samuel P. *The Clash of Civilizations and the Remaking of World Order* (New York, 1997)
Ives, Charles E. *Memos*, ed. John Kirkpatrick (London, 1973)
Jäger, Ludwig. *Seitenwechsel: Der Fall Schneider/Schwerte und die Diskretion der Germanistik* (Munich, 1998)
Jasper, Willi. *Der Bruder Heinrich Mann: Eine Biografie* (Munich, 1992)
——. *Faust und die Deutschen* (Berlin, 1998)
——. *Zauberberg Riva* (Berlin, 2011)
Jünger, Ernst. *Die totale Mobilmachung* (Berlin, 1931)
Keegan, John. *The First World War* (London, 2014)
Kennan, George F. *The Decline of Bismarck's European Order: Franco-Russian Relations 1873–1890* (Princeton, 1979)
Kinau, Jacob. *Der Kampf um die Seeherrschaft von der Hanse bis zum Weltkrieg* (Munich and Berlin, 1938)
Kjellén, Rudolf. *Die Ideen von 1914: Eine weltgeschichtliche Perspektive* (Leipzig, 1915)
Koenen, Gerd. *Unheilige Allianz: Rußland und Deutschland. Eine 400-jährige Faszination in Freundschaft und Feindschaft* (Frankfurt, 1990)
Koldau, Linda Maria. *The Titanic on Film: Myth versus Truth* (New York, 2012)
Korff, Hermann August. *Faustischer Glaube* (Leipzig, 1938)
Kramer, Alan. *Dynamic of Destruction: Culture and Mass Killing in the First World War* (Oxford, 2007)
Kraus, Karl. *The Last Days of Mankind*, trans. Fred Bridgman and Edward Timms (New Haven, 2015)
Krockow, Christian von. *Die Deutschen in ihrem Jahrhundert 1890–1990* (Reinbek, 1990)
Kroll, Frank-Lothar. *Geburt der Moderne: Politik, Gesellschaft und Kultur vor dem Ersten Weltkrieg* (Berlin, 2013)

Lankheit, Klaus (ed.). *Wassily Kandinsky / Franz Marc: Briefwechsel* (Munich, 1983)
Leonhard, Jörn. *Die Büchse der Pandora* (Munich, 2014)
Leppmann, Wolfgang. *Goethe und die Deutschen: Der Nachruhm eines Dichters im Wandel der Zeit und der Weltanschauungen. Ein Spiegelbild deutscher Kultur und Bildung* (Berne and Munich, 1982)
Liebeschütz, Hans and Paucker, Arnold (eds). *Das Judentum in der deutschen Umwelt 1800–1850* (Tübingen, 1977)
Liebknecht, Karl. *Ausgewählte Reden und Aufsätze* (Berlin, 1952)
——. *Gesammelte Reden und Schriften*, 9 vols (Berlin, 1958–74)
Linthout, Ine van. *Das Buch in der nationalsozialistischen Propagandapolitik* (Berlin, 2012)
Ludendorff, Erich von. *Meine Kriegserinnerungen 1914–1918* (Berlin, 1919)
——. *Der totale Krieg* (Munich, 1935)
Mac Orlan, Pierre and Bofa, Gus. *U-713 ou Les gentilshommes d'infortune* (Paris, 1917)
Mann, Golo. *Der Geist Amerikas* (Stuttgart, 1954)
——. *The History of Germany since 1789*, trans. Marian Jackson (London, 1968)
——. '1914 1939 Der Zweite Weltkrieg war die Wiederholung des Ersten', *Die Zeit* (14 August 1964)
Mann, Heinrich. *Ein Zeitalter wird besichtigt: Erinnerungen* (Frankfurt, 1988)
——. *Macht und Mensch: Essays* (Frankfurt, 1989)
——. *Studienausgabe in Einzelbänden*, ed. Peter-Paul Schneider, 27 vols (Frankfurt, 1987–2011)
Mann, Thomas. *Aufsätze, Reden, Essays*, ed. Harry Matter, 3 vols (Berlin and Weimar, 1983–6)
——. *Briefe*, ed. Erika Mann (Frankfurt, 1979)
——. *Essays II: Für das neue Deutschland 1919–1925* (Frankfurt, 1993)
——. *Große kommentierte Frankfurter Ausgabe: Werke, Briefe, Tagebücher*, ed. Heinrich Detering and others, 38 vols (Frankfurt, 2002—)
——. *Reflections of a Nonpolitical Man*, trans. Walter D. Morris (New York, 1983)
Mann, Thomas and Mann, Heinrich. *Briefwechsel 1900–1949*, ed. Hans Wysling (Frankfurt, 1959); *Letters of Heinrich and Thomas Mann, 1900–1949*, ed. Hans Wysling, trans. Don Reneau (Berkeley and London, 1998)
Marc, Franz. *Briefe aus dem Felde*, ed. Klaus Lankheit (Munich, 1982)
Marder, Arthur J. *From the Dreadnought to Scapa Flow: The Royal Navy in the Fisher Era 1904–1919*, 5 vols (London, 1961–70)
Marinetti, Filippo Tommaso. *Selected Writings*, ed. R. W. Flint (London, 1971)
Mayer, Hans. *Ein Deutscher auf Widerruf: Erinnerungen I* (Frankfurt, 1988)
Meinecke, Friedrich. *The German Catastrophe: Reflections and Recollections*, trans. Sidney B. Fay (Cambridge, Mass., 1950)
Mesenhöller, Mathias. 'Schlacht um England: Als Spaniens Armada in die Katastrophe segelte', *Spiegel-Online* (17 August 2008)
Meyer, Henry Cord. *Mitteleuropa in German Thoughts and Action 1815–1945* (The Hague, 1955)
Moeller van den Bruck, Arthur. *Das Dritte Reich* (Berlin, 1923)
——. Introduction to F. M. Dostojewski, *Sämtliche Werke*, 22 vols (Munich, 1922)

Mommsen, Wolfgang J. *War der Kaiser an allem schuld? Wilhelm II. und die preußisch-deutschen Machteliten* (Munich, 2002)
Mühsam, Erich. *Tagebücher*, ed. Chris Hirte and Conrad Piens, 15 vols (Berlin, 2011—)
——. *Das seid ihr Hunde wert! Ein Lesebuch*, ed. Markus Liske and Manja Präkels (Berlin, 2014)
Münkler, Herfried. *Der große Krieg: Die Welt 1914–1918* (Reinbeck, 2013)
Neitzel, Sönke. *Weltkrieg und Revolution 1914–1918/19* (Berlin, 2008)
Niemöller, Martin. *From U-Boat to Pulpit* (Chicago and New York, 1937)
Nietzsche, Friedrich. *Untimely Meditations*, trans. R. J. Hollingdale (Cambridge, 1983)
Noske, Gustav. *Von Kiel bis Kapp: Zur Geschichte der deutschen Revolution* (Berlin, 1920)
Owen, Wilfred. *Poems of War* (London, 1989)
Pemsel, Helmut. *Seeherrschaft*, ii: *Eine maritime Weltgeschichte von der Dampfschiffahrt bis zur Gegenwart* (Augsburg, 1995)
Piper, Ernst. *Nacht über Europa: Kulturgeschichte des Ersten Weltkriegs* (Berlin, 2013)
Plenge, Johann. *1789 und 1914: Die symbolischen Jahre in der Geschichte des politischen Geistes* (Berlin, 1916)
Quadflieg, Will. *Wir spielen immer: Erinnerungen* (Frankfurt, 1976)
Rauschning, Hermann. *Hitler Speaks: A Series of Political Conversations with Adolf Hitler on his Real Aims* (London, 1939)
Reemtsma, Jan Philipp. 'Die Idee des Vernichtungskrieges: Clausewitz–Ludendorff–Hitler', *Vernichtungskrieg, Verbrechen der Wehrmacht 1941–1944*, ed. Hannes Heer and Klaus Naumann (Hamburg, 1995)
Riezler, Kurt. *Tagebücher, Aufsätze und Dokumente*, ed. Karl Dietrich Erdmann (Göttingen, 1972)
Ritter, Gerhard. *Staatskunst und Kriegshandwerk: Das Problem des 'Militarismus' in Deutschland*, 4 vols (Munich, 1954–68)
Ritterbusch, Paul. *Demokratie und Diktatur: Über Wesen und Wirklichkeit des westeuropäischen Parteienstaates* (Berlin and Vienna, 1939)
——. 'Hochschule und Wissenschaft im Kriege', *Kieler Blätter* (1940), 1–15
Röhl, John C. G. 'Deutschlands "erhebliche Verantwortung" für 1914', *Die Welt* (21 October 2011)
——. 'Kaiser Wilhelm II. und der deutsche Antisemitismus', *Vorurteil und Völkermord: Entwicklungslinien des Antisemitismus*, ed. Wolfgang Benz and Werner Bergmann (Freiburg, 1997)
——. 'Wie Deutschland 1914 den Krieg plante', *Süddeutsche Zeitung* (5 March 2014)
Rolland, Romain. *Journal des années de guerre, 1914–1919: Notes et documents pour servir à l'histoire morale de l'Europe de ce temps*, ed. Maria Romain Rolland (Paris, 1952)
——. *Correspondance Romain Rolland / Stefan Zweig*, ed. Jean-Yves Brancy (Paris, 2014—) (two volumes published to date covering the years 1910–19 and 1919–27)
Rosenberg, Alfred. *The Myth of the Twentieth Century*, trans. James B. Whisker (Newport Beach, 1982)
Rösler, Ute. *Die Titanic und die Deutschen: Mediale Repräsentation und gesellschaftliche Wirkung eines Mythos* (Bielefeld, 2013)

Rostron, Sir Arthur Henry. *Home from the Sea* (London, 1931) (republished in 2011 as *Titanic Hero: The Autobiography of Captain Rostron of the 'Carpathia'*)
Rothacker, Erich. *Die Kriegswichtigkeit der Philosophie* (Bonn, 1944)
Rudloff, Holger. 'Ocean Steamships, Hansa, Titanic: Die drei Ozeandampfer in Thomas Manns Roman "Der Zauberberg"', *Thomas Mann-Jahrbuch*, xviii (2005), 243–64
Scheer, Reinhold. *Deutschlands Hochseeflotte im Weltkrieg: Persönliche Erinnerungen 1915–1943* (Berlin, n.d.)
Scheler, Max. *Der Genius des Kriegs und der Deutsche Krieg* (Leipzig, 1915)
Schirrmacher, Frank. 'Hitlers Code: Holocaust aus faustischem Streben? Daniel Jonah Goldhagens Remythisierung der Deutschen', *Frankfurter Allgemeine Zeitung* (15 April 1996)
Schivelbusch, Wolfgang. *Die Bibliothek von Löwen* (Munich and Vienna, 1988)
Schneider, Hans Ernst. 'Stalingrad und das Tragische', *Das Reich* (7 February 1943)
Scholz, Rüdiger. *Die beschädigte Seele des großen Mannes: Goethes Faust* (Würzburg, 2011)
Schröder, Joachim. *Die U-Boote des Kaisers: Die Geschichte des deutschen U-Boot-Krieges gegen Großbritannien im Ersten Weltkrieg* (Berlin, 2003)
Schubert, Dietrich. *Künstler im Trommelfeuer des Kriegs 1914–18* (Heidelberg, 2013)
Schwabe, Klaus. *Wissenschaft und Kriegsmoral: Die deutschen Hochschullehrer und die politischen Grundlagen des Ersten Weltkrieges* (Göttingen, 1969)
Schwabe, Toni (ed.). *Johann Wolfgang von Goethe: Der Tragödie Faust erster Teil. Erster Band der deutschen Kriegsbibliothek* (Jena, 1915)
See, Klaus von. *Barbar, Germane, Arier: Die Suche nach der Identität der Deutschen* (Heidelberg, 1994)
Sombart, Werner. *Händler und Helden* (Munich and Leipzig, 1915)
Speer, Albert. *Inside the Third Reich: Memoirs*, trans. Richard and Clara Winston (London, 1970)
Straub, Eberhard. *Albert Ballin: Der Reeder des Kaisers* (Berlin, 2011)
Süselbeck, Jan. 'Der Teufel blieb aus', www.literaturkritik.de (12 December 2008)
Thoß, Bruno and Volkmann, Hans-Erich (eds). *Erster Weltkrieg–Zweiter Weltkrieg: Krieg, Kriegserlebnis, Kriegserfahrung in Deutschland 1914–1945* (Paderborn, 2002)
Tirpitz, Alfred von. *Erinnerungen* (Leipzig, 1919)
Troeltsch, Ernst. *Glaube und Sitte in unserem großen Kriege* (Berlin, 1914)
——. *Der Kulturkrieg* (Berlin, 1916)
Tucholsky, Kurt. *Fromme Gesänge* (Charlottenburg, 1919)
——. *Gesamtausgabe: Texte und Briefe*, 22 vols (Reinbek 1996—)
Ullrich, Volker. *Die nervöse Großmacht 1871–1918: Aufstieg und Untergang des deutschen Kaiserreichs* (Frankfurt, 1997)
——. 'Nun schlittern sie wieder', *Die Zeit* (24 January 2014)
——. *Hitler: Ascent 1889–1939*, trans. Jefferson Chase (London, 2016)
Valentiner, Max. *300.000 Tonnen versenkt! Meine U-Bootfahrten* (Berlin and Vienna, 1917)
——. *U 38 – Wikingerfahrten eines deutschen U-Bootes* (Berlin, 1934) (republished in 2002 as *Todesgefahr über uns: U 38 im Einsatz*)

Wegner, Bernd. *Hitlers politische Soldaten: Die Waffen-SS 1933–1945. Studien zu Leitbild, Struktur und Funktion einer nationalsozialistischen Elite* (Paderborn, 1982)

Wehler, Hans-Ulrich. *Das Deutsche Kaiserreich 1871–1918* (Göttingen, 1977) (Deutsche Geschichte ix)

Wiborg, Susanne. 'Deutschlands "Titanic": Eine Erinnerung an den "Imperator", das deutsche "Überschiff", und die Zeit, als Luxusliner nationale Triumphe waren', *Die Zeit* (8 April 1999)

Wilamowitz-Moellendorf, Ulrich von. *Reden aus der Kriegszeit* (Berlin, 1915)

Willing, Martin. 'Stummel, Friedrich. Kevelaers bedeutender Künstler (1850–1919)', *Blattus Martini: Kevelaer Enzyklopädie*, http://www.blattus.de/kaz/texte/s_kaz/stummel-friedrich. html

Winkler, Heinrich August. '1914 und 1939: Die Kontinuität der Kriegspartei', *Frankfurter Allgemeine Zeitung* (25 August 2014)

——. 'Die Oktoberreform', *Frankfurter Allgemeine Zeitung* (1 June 2014)

——. 'Was nicht zerbricht', *Die Zeit* (1 October 2014)

——. *The Age of Catastrophe*, trans. Stewart Spencer (New Haven, 2015)

Wolff, Theodor. *Tagebücher 1914–1919*, ed. Bernd Sösemann, 2 vols (Boppard, 1984)

Wolz, Nicolas. *'Und wir verrosten in den Häfen': Deutschland, Großbritannien und der Krieg zur See 1914–1918* (Munich, 2013)

Wundt, Wilhelm. 'England und der Krieg', *Internationale Monatsschrift für Wissenschaft, Kunst und Technik*, ix (1914/15), 121–8

Wyatt, Horace. *Malice in Kulturland* (London, 1914)

Zweig, Stefan. *The World of Yesterday: An Autobiography* (New York, 1943)

Illustration Credits

1. Wikimedia Commons. 2. Verlagsarchiv. 3. Library of Congress. 4. Library of Congress. 5. Wikimedia Commons. 6. Library of Congress. 7. Verlagsarchiv. 8. Library of Congress. 9. Verlagsarchiv. 10. Bundesarchiv (Bild 183-R35451). 11. Wikimedia Commons. 12. Deutsche Nationalbibliothek. 13. Verlagsarchiv. 14. Bundesarchiv (Bild 134-C1831). 15. Wikimedia Commons. 16. Verlagsarchiv. 17. Bundesarchiv (Bild 102-03343A). 18. Mauritius Images. 19. Wikimedia Commons. 20–28. Verlagsarchiv. 29. Bundesarchiv (Bild 183-R98911). 30. Verlagsarchiv. 31. Museo Nacional Centro de Arte Reina Sofia.

Index